Reach For The Firefighter Badge!

How To Master The Fire Department Entry-Level Testing Process

STEVE PRZIBOROWSKI

Because of the dynamic nature of the Internet, any web addresses or links contained in
this book may have changed since publication and may no longer be valid. The views
expressed in this work are solely those of the author and do not necessarily reflect the
views of the publisher, and the publisher hereby disclaims any responsibility for them.

Any people depicted in stock imagery provided by Thinkstock are models,
and such images are being used for illustrative purposes only.
Certain stock imagery © Thinkstock.

Lulu Publishing Services rev. date: 11/05/2013

Table of Contents

Foreword

It has been my distinct pleasure and honor to know and work with Steve Prziborowski for many years, through his position in Santa Clara County, his involvement with the International Association of Fire Chiefs and through his teaching, coaching and mentoring of firefighters.

Steve has a tremendous passion for helping new firefighters get their start in this highly rewarding profession. There is no doubt it is a highly competitive process to get hired as a firefighter. Serious candidates need a competitive edge and *Reach for the Firefighter Badge* is how you get the edge. I wish this "how to get hired" playbook existed when I was trying to get my start into the fire service.

During my 22-year tenure as a fire chief I have interviewed hundreds of young men and women for firefighter positions. Some candidates were well prepared and it showed throughout the process. Unfortunately, many of the candidates were woefully underprepared. Based on their dismal performance during the hiring process, it was painful to watch them eliminate themselves from consideration.

In most instances, a candidate's poor performance during the hiring process is completely avoidable. Candidates need to know the process and how to master it. Steve's book is a treasure trove of knowledge for the aspiring firefighter. Don't leave something as critical as getting your career started to chance.

Steve is an extremely talented and motivated leader, author and speaker. If you enjoy Steve's books, I strongly recommend his live programs. There he shares more best practices, tips and advice to help you get hired into this amazing career.

If you're fortunate enough to have your career started, I would encourage you to look to Steve as a resource to help you prepare for promotion. His experience is invaluable and his passion for helping officer candidates get promoted is unsurpassed.

Fire Chief (ret.) Richard B. Gasaway, PhD, EFO, CFO
Chief Scientist, Public Safety Laboratory
Founder, Situational Awareness Matters!

Preface

This book is meant to pick up where my previous book, "The Future Firefighter's Preparation Guide," left off. It is meant to complement the information within that book, and take your preparation to the next level. This book primarily focuses on the firefighter testing process; also known as the firefighter hiring process, and how to be the best you can be to be successful.

Thousands may start the hiring process, but very few are fortunate enough to be selected as firefighters. Within this book are numerous "nuggets" or "key points" you can use to help yourself be unique and be the best you can be during the hiring process and upon getting hired as a firefighter. Too many candidates focus on trying too hard to have the best resume, when in fact there is no such thing as the best resume. When I was testing for the position of firefighter, I made that same mistake. I focused too hard on trying to jam pack my resume with training, experience, education or other accomplishment when in fact I should have been focusing on how to best sell or market those key personal character traits I possessed to the fire department who was evaluating me in their hiring process.

Remember the phrase "hire for character and attitude, train for skills." What that means is that we can train many (not all) to become a firefighter. However, we cannot teach you to have a great attitude and we cannot teach you those key character traits that are successful to be a firefighter. Your parents or your guardians who raised you, not to mention the friends you hang out with, should have instilled all of those character traits in you. If nothing else, you should have been smart enough to pick out the good character traits by watching and learning from others. Fire departments hire people, not resumes. We want to hire people that will fit into our culture and represent us in a very positive manner!

Acknowledgments

This book could not have been published without the assistance and support of many individuals over the course of my life and my career.

To my first family: my wife and my best friend Bonnie. I could not have done this without your love and your support. You allow me to do all those things I enjoy doing. In turn, I want you to know how much I love you, and that I don't take all that you do for me for granted. I'll be forever grateful for all that you do for our family and me.

To my second family: the fire service. Thank you for allowing me the honor and the privilege of serving with you.

To all of the men and women at the greatest Fire Department in the World: the Santa Clara County Fire Department. I consider myself extremely fortunate to be able to serve you each day to the best of my ability. To Fire Chief Ken Kehmna, and Assistant Chief Don Jarvis (the best bosses I have worked for), and to the rest of our A-Staff (Administrative Staff) team, all of who make up the best A-Staff team I could ever imagine having the pleasure to work for and work with: thank you for your support. To all of the incredible personnel I am fortunate enough to serve within the Training Division, both past and present: you make my day being yourself and doing what you do, each and every day, which includes putting up with me.

To my buddies from the very beginning twenty-some years ago as we made our minds up to go full speed ahead into becoming a firefighter: Andy Pestana (Firefighter – South San Francisco Fire Department,

California), Ron Phillips (Engineer – Sacramento Metropolitan Fire District, California), and Greg Vitz (Captain – Stockton Fire Department, California); you guys are the best. Through thick and thin we stuck together and did what we had to do to ensure our dreams became a reality.

To my friends, role models, and mentors: I cannot even start to thank you for all that you have done to assist me throughout my career. There are so many people that have assisted me throughout my career that I could not even start to list everyone.

To everyone at the Chabot College Fire Technology Program: I am proud to be associated with such a great fire technology program that does so much to prepare our future and current firefighters for success. Bob Buell, Ricky Hurtado, John Torres, Jeff Zolfarelli, Derek Krause, Klaus Zalinskis, John McPartland, Rich Brown, John Whiting, Mary Pastore, John McInnis, Gary Centoni, Mark Bennett, and Jeff Urnes: all of you are the best at what you do, keep up the great work!

To Craig Allyn Rose of Craig Allyn Rose Photography: you are one of the best fire department photographers I have ever seen. Thank you for allowing me to use your pictures and for all that you do to support the fire departments within Santa Clara County.

To everyone at Fire Engineering & FDIC: Bobby Halton, Diane Rothschild, Mary Jane Dittmar, and Ginger Mendolia, just to name a few – thanks for your support and for allowing me to be a part of Fire Engineering & FDIC.

To everyone at Firehouse Magazine & Firehouse Events: Harvey Eisner, Pete Matthews, Jeff Barrington, Scott Bieda, Greg Toritto, Ed Nichols & Tom Tobiason, just to name a few - thanks for your support and for allowing me to be a part of Firehouse Magazine, Firehouse.com and the various Firehouse Events (World, Expo and Central).

To everyone at Fire Rescue Magazine: Tim Sendelbach, Janelle Foskett & Shannon Pieper – thanks for your support and for allowing me to be a part of Fire Rescue Magazine.

To everyone at Fire Alumni: Bob Atlas, Brian Helmick and Judon Cherry, just to name a few – thanks for your support and for allowing me to be a part of Fire Alumni.

To Tony Vitalie at FireRecruit.com and Careers in the Fire Service – thanks for your support and for allowing me to be a part of FireRecruit.com.

To Craig Freeman at FireCareers.com and The Perfect Firefighter Candidate – thanks for your support and for allowing me to be a part of FireCareers.com.

To the Executive Boards of the Northern California and the Southern California Training Officers Association, past and present – thanks for your support and for allowing me to continue to assist you in your pursuit of furthering training and safety needs for our firefighters, whether it is sending out training information each week or teaching at the annual Fresno Symposium.

To the International Association of Fire Chiefs Program Planning Committee & Council Members – thanks for your support and for allowing me to be a part of Fire-Rescue International.

Last, but definitely not least, to all of our brothers and sisters who have made the ultimate sacrifice and have given their lives during the protection of lives and property: I will do my best to never forget you and to continue to learn from each tragedy in order to share the lessons learned with others, in order to help reduce future line-of-duty-deaths from occurring. This includes my buddy, Santa Clara County Fire Department Captain Mark McCormack, who paid the ultimate price on February 13, 2005 when he died in the line of duty during a structure fire in Los Gatos, California. Rest In Peace Brother.

CHAPTER 1

An Overview of The Fire Service Testing Process

Most companies typically do not hire everyone that asks for a job. Yes, there are exceptions, but they are rare. Governmental agencies, such as fire departments and police departments, tend to have the most different and numerous phases of a testing or hiring process, while private businesses do not. It is not uncommon to walk into a fast food restaurant or other service industry business and see job applications on the counter. Some of these are two-sided, and some are as simple as filling out a few items about yourself (name, address, phone number, last job worked). I've seen fast food restaurants that actually post a sign saying that they do job interviews every day during a certain time frame.

Somebody could walk into the restaurant, take a couple of minutes to complete the application, give it to a manager to review, and then in a couple of minutes, sit down for an oral interview with the manager. If successful, that oral interview could lead to a job offer, less than 30 minutes after you first filled that application out! Of course, they might take the time to do some reference checks, but then again they might not. It all depends on how desperate they are and how thorough they are. Now, don't think becoming a firefighter will be that easy. It is not uncommon to fill out an application and then have to wait 6 months to 4 years later to actually start your first day on the job! Even the most efficient fire departments typically take at least 4 months from the time you turn your application in to the first day of the academy. Part of the reason it takes so long to hire a firefighter is because we are the government, and things can take longer than what seems necessary at times (even to us that work for the fire departments).

The main reason it takes so long to hire a firefighter is because there are so many different phases of the firefighter hiring process that a person must successfully go through, just to make it to the recruit academy. Then, don't think you're on easy street just yet. You still have to successfully complete the recruit academy and then probation. Not easy, but it can be done. What one department requires it's candidates to go through in the way of the hiring process differs from jurisdiction to jurisdiction, and state-to-state.

Some of the most common phases of the firefighter hiring process you may encounter are:

- Recruitment Period / Application Filing Period
- Application Screening Process
- Written Examination
- Physical Ability Test
- Oral Interview
- Skills Assessment Test
- Fire Chief's Interview
- Background Investigation
- Conditional Job offer!
- Medical Examination
- Psychological Examination
- Polygraph Evaluation
- Recruit Academy
- Probation Period

NOTE: Testing process components can vary from department to department. I will provide more information on most of the typical testing components in more depth throughout this book.

# # # #

How Do I Find Out Which Fire Departments Are Hiring?

Getting hired as a firefighter is not a simple process. It is not as easy as going down to your local fire station, filling out an application, and getting told to report to duty the next day. While that may have occurred in some departments many years ago, it doesn't quite work that way today. It actually can take a great deal of research to find out which fire departments are accepting applications, and what their testing process entails. Becoming a firefighter is not easy, but if you spend some quality time researching the position and the entire testing process, your chances should increase greatly at obtaining that badge you have been coveting.

When I started taking firefighter tests, I figured all I had to do was keep my eyes on the Sunday newspaper and subscribe to one of the services that used to send you postcards (before the Internet) when departments are testing. That was a good start; however, I soon learned there was more to it than that.

While there are many people that just do those two things (which are actually good things to be doing, don't get me wrong), I think you can greatly increase your chances by searching or investigating as many of the following things as you can:

- **Newspapers.** Over the last ten to twenty years, primarily because of the Internet, it is extremely rare to see firefighter job openings in the local newspapers. Because of that reason, don't spend all of your time just waiting for a position to appear in the paper. If a fire department is going to advertise, it will usually be in the Sunday paper of a major city. If you go to the local public library on Monday morning, you can usually find many of the major nationwide newspapers there to view, free of charge. Another place to check for major city newspapers is large newsstands and major bookstore chains, which usually carry a large variety of newspapers and magazines.

3

- **Internet subscription services.** There are numerous subscription services available on the Internet that will provide nationwide testing information for under $100.00 per year. Not a bad investment when you think of it. I suggest not relying on just one service, but to subscribe to multiple services. I used to subscribe to two different services and found out the true value to having not one service, but two. Some services find out testing information before the others do, and vice-versa. Originally I had only subscribed to just one service. After talking with friends that subscribed to different services, I discovered that each service had their own benefits to offer, and that they each complemented each other.

  Two of the best services I have found that provide fire service employment opportunities include:

  1. **The Perfect Firefighter Candidate—**
     http://www.firecareers.com
     Are you looking for a career in the fire service or maybe you're interested in promoting? Perfect Firefighter Candidate (PFC) has been committed to helping individuals obtain their career goals since 1981. This is a National fire department recruitment service, and covers recruiting for all levels from firefighter to fire chief. Each time a department is accepting applications, PFC will notify you via email.

  2. **Careers in the Fire Service—**
     http://www.firerecruit.com
     They provide the most up-to-date and comprehensive employment information for nationwide fire recruitments. They post all fire careers from entry level firefighter, EMT and paramedic jobs to advanced promotional opportunities such as battalion chief and fire chief on their website. Their website is updated daily with new firefighter positions for municipal, state, federal, and even private fire agencies.

- **Firehouse.com website Jobs section.** In addition to the two above Internet subscription services, here is another valuable service that promises to advertise positions nationwide. This website is hosted by Firehouse Magazine, one of the most popular fire service trade publications. For more information, visit their website at http://www.firehouse.com

- **Networking.** By having a network of friends that are all taking firefighter tests, you will hopefully hear of a testing opportunity and then pass it on to the others. If you know of a testing opportunity, share it with your friends. You will then hope they do the same for you at some point. Remember, you're competing against the other candidates in some capacity, but you only truly compete against yourself. You are the one that has to perform throughout all phases of the hiring process. When I was testing, there was a group of about four of us that were doing as much as we could to better prepare ourselves for becoming firefighters. We would share information, trade off commuting to tests, commuting to visit fire stations, commuting to classes, etc. Besides gaining quality friends that will hopefully last a lifetime, we were all benefiting by learning something from each of us, based on our successes and failures.

- **Taking fire courses at the local community college or seminars offered through fire associations.** Most, if not all of the fire instructors are still working in the fire service. Many of them are aware of testing opportunities and share them with the classes. You also get a chance to network with other candidates, and best of all, increase your education level while adding something beneficial to your resume.

- **Fire trade publication classified sections.** Fire service trade publications, such as Firehouse Magazine, occasionally have entry-level firefighter positions advertised. Subscribing to many of these publications not only educates you on the past, present, and future of the fire service, but also exposes you to any available positions that might be advertised.

- **City or County Human Resource / Personnel Offices.** Many people are not aware that the fire department themselves are usually not the one that puts on a firefighter examination. It is usually the city or county human resource or personnel office. The names "human resource" and "personnel office" are usually synonymous. Every city and county has an office with either name that handles the testing for all of the city or county agencies within that jurisdiction such as the fire department, law enforcement, public works, recreational services, etc. The fire department usually informs the human resources / personnel office that they need to hold a firefighter exam and then it is usually scheduled around all of the other examinations that are occurring.
- **Companies that fire departments use to coordinate their testing process.** For lack of a better phrase, there are a number of companies out there who offer their services to fire departments. These services can range from recruiting candidates, to accepting and processing the applications, to facilitating a portion of the testing process such as the written examination, to ultimately creating the eligibility list that a fire department can hand select candidates to interview and/or put their screening process. The benefits for the candidate can include the ability to take one test or file one application and be eligible to apply or compete for positions with numerous fire departments in a regional area or around the country.

  Examples of such companies can include:
  1. **National Testing Network—** http://nationaltestingnetwork.com
  2. **Firehire—**http://www.firehire.com

While all of the above mentioned items are all of value when it comes to finding out who is testing, contacting each human resources / personnel office directly is probably your best method of finding out who is testing!

Remember, you must be in control of your own destiny! Don't expect to rely on others for information! If you do, you might miss out on that important test you have been waiting for!

While all of the above items are extremely important at assisting you in finding out which fire departments are currently testing, I sincerely believe the most important item is to do your own research and actually be proactive in your search. All of the above items are being reactive, because you are waiting for someone to give you some information. That is not necessarily bad. I think of the above items as "back-up plans" to assist you in finding positions. Back up plans are necessary for almost everything we do in life, especially when it comes to achieving the dream of becoming a firefighter. To better organize all of this information you are going to be soon obtaining, I recommend getting a binder with some blank paper. This will be the storage location for the information that you obtain during your research. If you are extremely computer literate, then by all means feel free to develop a spreadsheet or database of some form or fashion. However, I prefer the binder because you can keep it with you at all times since it is portable.

CHAPTER 2

The Firefighter Job Flyer

The job flyer is the announcement that is sent out by the fire department, a private recruitment company, the personnel department, or the human resources department; whoever is responsible for hosting and delivering the firefighter examination for the respective jurisdiction. The job flyer is usually one to two pages in length, and covers all of the basic "w" information:

- Who—is eligible to apply.
- When—you must apply by, when the testing dates are for the process, etc.
- What—the minimum and desirable qualifications may be, what the duties and responsibilities of the position are, what you need to do to apply for the position, and what wages and benefits are offered as part of the position.
- Where—you must apply.
- Why—you should consider applying (information is typically provided about the department as well as the community).

Many candidates do not take the time to really read and digest the job flyer, and that is a shame. Everything on the flyer is important and relevant; not reading everything puts you at risk for:

- Missing out on important information
- Failing to follow all of the directions

- Assuming you know what they are looking for
- Not understanding what they are looking for in a candidate
- Not understanding what the job entails
- Not understanding all of their expectations

Besides reading the job flyer completely, make sure you make a copy of it for your file that you will create on this department you are testing for. Include in this file copies of your application, resume, correspondence received from the department, notes on your research from visiting fire stations, surfing the Internet, etc.

# # # #

Sample Firefighter Job Flyer #1

THE CHABOT FIRE DEPARTMENT
IS HIRING FIREFIGHTERS!

COME WORK FOR A PREMIERE FIRE DEPARTMENT IN A PREMIERE CITY . . .

We invite you to start a REWARDING career as a Firefighter with our City! Our Fire Department is dedicated to protecting the community and providing for life safety, environmental protection, and property conservation through education, hazard reduction, and emergency response.

REQUIREMENTS

Age: Must be at least 21 years of age by final filing date of June 4, and show proof of age at the time of the Written Test.

Smoking: Must be a non-smoker; smoking on or off duty is prohibited.

E.M.T. New employees must obtain a California Emergency Medical Technician 1 Certificate prior to the completion of probation (the first year of employment following Academy training).

Education: Equivalent to graduation from high school.

License: Valid driver's license. Must obtain a Firefighter Restricted Class B license prior to the completion of probation.

Medical: Must meet NFPA Standard 1582, "Medical Requirements for Fire Fighters."

EXAMPLES OF DUTIES

For a comprehensive list of duties for Firefighter, and more information about our Department, go to our website—click "Job Opportunities," then click "Job Descriptions."

SPECIAL NOTES

After the Written Test used in this selection process, successful candidates must qualify on a physical ability test, department oral interview(s), background investigation (including polygraph), psychological exam, and medical exam prior to selection. The requirement to participate in the physical ability test will be waived for candidates who submit proof of a currently valid PAT or CPAT certificate by **Tuesday, June 4.**

SALARY

All candidates for Firefighter will be initially hired into the temporary position of Fire Trainee while assigned to the Training Academy (approximately 11 weeks). During training, Recruits are paid $3,758/month plus a City contribution of up to $695/month for family health care coverage. Upon graduation, Firefighters are paid $3758-$4,568/month (base pay) PLUS full benefits listed below, as well as any applicable premiums.

SALARY STRUCTURE

- $4141/month max. upon shift assignment after training period ($3758/month plus 7% Haz Mat First Responder Premium of $263/month plus EMT Premium of $120/month if applicable)

- $4342/month max. at start of Month 7 ($3946/month plus 7% Haz Mat First Responder Premium of $276/month plus EMT Premium of $120/month if applicable)
- $4553/month max. at start of Year 2 (end of 12-month Probation Period) ($4143/month plus 7% Haz Mat First Responder Premium of $290/month plus EMT Premium of $120/month if applicable)
- Educational Incentive Pay at start of Year 2 of up to 9% (up to $373/month) if applicable

BENEFIT HIGHLIGHTS

Notable benefits specific to Firefighters include:

- 100% City-paid PERS retirement using 3% @ 50 formula
- Premium Pay for Special Assignments: Paramedic—up to 19%; Haz Mat Team—up to 13%
- 48/96 Schedule (Mandatory)

APPLICATION PROCEDURE

Candidates must submit a scantron application form. Applications are currently available, but cannot be submitted until May 4. To obtain an application, please call (555) 555-5555, or e-mail iwantanapplication@cityofchabot.com

Applications will be accepted beginning Tuesday, May 4 at 7:30 a.m. The Application deadline is 5:30 P.M. Tuesday, June 4, or when 2,000 applications have been filed, whichever comes first. Applications of past and present Fire Department auxiliaries are automatically accepted. Auxiliaries must apply in person on or after May 4, after 7:30 a.m.

ONLY 2,000 APPLICATIONS WILL BE ACCEPTED at:

City of Chabot—Personnel Building, 1234 Chabot Blvd., Chabot, California 91111

SELECTION PROCESS

The examination will consist of a Written Test, weighted 100%, covering a range of skills and abilities that are important for the job. Handouts detailing online practice test information will be available at the Personnel Building following the sessions. The Written Test is published by Ergometrics.

Testing will take place on Wednesday, June 29. Three test sessions will be conducted at the Marriott Hotel in Chabot. Candidates will have a choice of test session appointment times at the time of application. Candidates with disabilities who require special testing arrangements must contact the Personnel Department.

# # # #

Sample Firefighter Job Flyer #2

Firefighter Employment Opportunity—City of Acme

Monthly Salary Range—$4,207-$5,114
Final Filing Date: 4:30 pm, Friday August 15

THE POSITION

Under supervision, responds to fire alarms and other emergency calls for the protection of life and property; renders first aid and lifesaving assistance; participates in fire prevention and training activities; performs fire fighting and fire station equipment maintenance. Examples of duties include, but are not limited to performing fire control activities and utilizing strategies in the areas of victim rescue; exposure tactics; ventilation; fire containment and extinguishment; fights structural, residential, commercial, industrial, chemical, vehicle and wildland fires; operates pumps, building heating and cooling systems, cutting, boring and sawing tools, lighting, lifting and air moving equipment, various types of extinguishers, appliances elevators, fire protection and escape systems, radio equipment and meters; uses a variety of tools, ropes, knots, ladders, lifelines, and belts; couples, reels, unreels and carries hoses; connects nozzles and valve fittings; extends and reduces hose lines; lays single and multiple hose lines; lays hoses and operates hose streams above and below street level; raises, climbs and works from extension ladders; makes forcible entries and transmits alarms; controls traffic; provides emergency care and treatment of patients; lifts, carries and transports patients; identifies common, special, structural and panic hazards; examines the storage, handling and use of flammable and combustible liquids and of other hazardous materials; makes recommendations regarding the correction of hazards; performs general maintenance work in the up-keep of the Fire Department property; operates computers and computer aided dispatch equipment; operates City vehicles and performs related work as required.

QUALIFICATIONS

MINIMUM TESTING REQUIREMENTS NOTE: These are entrance requirements to the competitive examination and do not assure a place on the eligibility list.

An applicant must be at least 18 years of age and have a high school diploma or its equivalent and possess either a record of training on official letterhead verifying training or a current certification by the State of California in at least one of the following categories by the Final Filing Date:

1. California State Fire Marshal Certified Firefighter I (FF-l) **OR;**
2. Proof of completion (provide Certified Training Record or Letter) of a training program necessary to obtain a FF-1 certificate **OR;**
3. Proof of satisfactory current attendance (provide letter from school) in a training program necessary to obtain a FF-1 certificate. The candidate must have their Fire Academy training **completed by December 31.**

The position also requires a California Emergency Medical Technician 1 (EMT) and possession of a valid California Driver's License with a good driving record.

EXAMINATION PROCESS

WRITTEN EXAMINATION—PASS/FAIL: A job-related written examination will be administered on, **September 20th and 21st,** to test the candidate's knowledge and abilities necessary for success as a Firefighter. The test may consist of a reading comprehension section and a general knowledge section which includes questions in the areas of reasoning ability, mechanical perception, mathematical ability, and ability to understand and comprehend written and oral instructions. Candidates must earn a passing score on the written examination to be eligible to advance to the physical agility test.

PHYSICAL AGILITY TEST—PASS/FAIL: Is scheduled during the week of October 17th. A limited number of candidates who pass the written examination will be invited to the physical agility test. Those candidates will be evaluated on their physical preparedness to perform a series of job-related events. A physical agility test will be given to test your ability to perform firefighting duties that require physical agility, strength, and endurance. Because this test is arduous, it is important, critical, and essential that you be in excellent physical condition. See your doctor and start training now! Additional examination dates may be scheduled if necessary.

ADDITIONAL TESTING INFORMATION Selected applicants will also be required to complete a polygraph exam and an extensive background investigation. Those who receive a conditional offer of employment will also be required to successfully complete a medical examination, a drug & alcohol screen, and a psychological evaluation before an offer is finalized. Individuals are urged not to resign current employment until a final written offer of employment is received, accepted, and processed.

BENEFITS

The City provides a deferred compensation plan; vacation days, increasing on 8th, 15th and 20th service anniversaries; 200 hours of paid holiday time in lieu of holiday time off; sick leave 12 hours per month including an incentive plan; 2.7%@57 retirement program through CalPERS; excellent health insurance that includes medical, prescription, dental, vision and employee assistance program coverage; and City-paid group life insurance of $25,000. The City does not participate in Social Security except as required for Medicare.

THE CITY OF IS AN EQUAL OPPORTUNITY EMPLOYER

This job flyer does not constitute a contract and its terms and conditions can change without notice.

# # # #

Sample Firefighter Job Flyer #3

City of Hometown, USA

BE A HERO!

Are you interested in being a part of a dynamic fire department equipped with state of the art apparatus and modern fire houses? Does working in collaboration with a team of dedicated professionals to provide top-notch service sound appealing? Then our City's Fire Department may be the place for you!

ENTRY LEVEL FIREFIGHTER/EMT or FIREFIGHTER/PARAMEDIC

The recruitment will remain open until 250 qualified applications have been received. Applicants are encouraged to apply early!

Firefighter/EMT or Firefighter/Paramedic positions:

Under general supervision, performs fire suppression, emergency medical assistance, and hazardous materials mitigation activities while maintaining the following core values:

Dedication: A passionate belief in the department mission, our personnel and our community.

Cooperation: Communication, team effort, respect towards others, openness.

Professionalism: Competency, commitment to quality and pride in our work

Integrity: Moral and intellectual honesty and accountability for our individual and collective activities.

Leadership: The ability to inspire, motivate and coach towards our common goal.

Respect: Recognizing that all that are encountered (community members, co-workers, members of outside agencies, and department personnel) have the right to be addressed in a courteous, sincere and professional manner.

Education and Experience Requirements:

The successful candidate will have any combination of education and/ or experience that has provided the knowledge, skills and abilities necessary for satisfactory job performance. A typical way to acquire the appropriate background includes:

- High school diploma or equivalent.
- Vocational training and college coursework in fire technology are highly desirable.

Licenses/Certificates/Special Requirements:

- Valid Class C California Driver's License.

- Ability to obtain and maintain a Valid Class B California Driver's License with tank endorsement by completion of the probationary period.
- Ability to obtain a California State Fire Marshal's Office Firefighter I certificate within the first year of the probationary period.
- Ability to obtain a California State Fire Marshal's Office Firefighter II certificate by the end of the probationary period.
- Ability to successfully complete the department's acting Engineer program by the end of the probationary period.
- Ability to successfully complete our Haz Mat program by the end of the probationary period.
- Vision requirements: Not less than 20/100 in each eye correctable to not less than 20/30 in each eye with glasses, without functional color-blindness or impairment. Limitations in the field of vision may be disqualifying.

EMT Additional Requirements:

- California EMT certificate or National Registry EMT certificate.
- CPR certificate

Paramedic Additional Requirements:

- California Paramedic license with current certifications in ACLS, PALS or PEPP, and PHTLS or BTLS.
- Paramedic accreditation with the County EMS Agency by the completion of the department's preceptor program that will occur during the probationary period.

Compensation and Benefits:

The annual salary is $76,384 to $92,835, depending on qualifications. Current benefit features include:

CalPERS Retirement Benefit:

- Classic Employees—3% @ 55 benefit, 3 year final average compensation.
- New Employees—2.7% @ 57 benefit, 3 year final average compensation.
- Required PERS contributions vary by plan. All required contributions are tax deferred.
- Cafeteria Benefits Plan for employees/dependents includes $1,620 monthly for medical and dental plans; childcare and medical expenses can be paid for with pre-tax dollars.

A complete benefit summary package can be found online at the City website.

This position is represented by the IAFF bargaining unit.

The probationary period for this position is twenty-four (24) months.

Application Instructions:

To be considered for this position, submit a completed City application, resume, proof of valid EMT and CPR, or Paramedic, CPAT card, and supplemental questionnaire either in person at City Hall or online through the City Human Resources website.

Selection Process:

The process will include the following steps:

1. Apply by submitting the following:
   a. An application, resume and supplemental questionnaire.
   b. A valid CPAT (Candidate Physical Ability Test) card. CPAT cards must be dated after May 15 of last year. For CPAT information, applications, test site locations, and registration, please visit http://www.cpatonline.org

    c. Current California EMT or National Registry EMT certificate and CPR certificates **OR** Current California Paramedic license and required certifications.

2. After you submit your application, you must take and successfully pass a written test through National Testing Network before May 3 of this year. To be considered passing, you must meet the following scores requirements: 70% combined score, 75% Video Score, 65% Mechanical Score and 70% Reading Score and Math Score. Test must be dated after May 15 of last year. For testing information, applications, test site locations and registration, please visit http://nationaltestingnetwork.com—once there select FIRE and choose our fire department.

3. RSVP and attend:
       a. Skills assessment for either EMT or Paramedic.
       b. Oral board interview (invitations for both will be emailed to you)

4. Placement on the Eligibility List—used to fill current openings as well as future openings generated within one year of list creation.

5. Successful completion of a comprehensive background investigation, fingerprints, psychological and medical evaluations are required for this position.

6. Fire Chief's interview.

Only those candidates who have the best combination of qualifications in relation to the requirements and duties of the position will continue in the selection process. Meeting the minimum qualifications does not guarantee an invitation to participate in the process.

Tentative Recruitment Schedule:

- First review of applications—April
- Skills Assessment and Oral Board Interviews—May
- Fire Chief Interviews—June

- Background Investigations—July
- Psychological Evaluations—August
- Medical Evaluations—August
- Recruit Academy—September through December

# # # #

Better Understanding The Firefighter Job Flyer

Have you ever read a firefighter job flyer and wondered what certain items meant and how (or if) they actually applied to you? If you have, you are probably not alone. The real key is what you have done to educate yourself about all of the portions of a firefighter testing process, the actual job description of a firefighter (for that specific department), and the wage and benefit packages that are being advertised for the specific position you are applying for.

When I turned in my first firefighter application, I really didn't spend a great deal of time evaluating the job flyer. About the only things I looked at were the minimum requirements (to make sure I was able to take the test), and the final filing date (to ensure that I got the application in on time to be considered). It didn't take me long to realize that there was a great deal of valuable information to be found on the job flyer. Information that could actually assist me in preparing for the department's testing process (including the oral interview), as well as educating me in how fire departments differ from each other based on their makeup, demographics, wage and benefit packages, and testing processes.

What type of information does the job flyer contain and why is it important to you, the firefighter candidate that is aspiring to work for that department?

Here are some of the main points to a job flyer and why you should pay attention to them:

Job Title:

This is the <u>exact</u> title that the agency is recruiting for. This exact title should go in the objective portion of your resume (the first heading underneath your personal contact information – name, address, and phone number). This title will also be required for the application. Make sure you are familiar with that job title. Countless candidates come by the fire station and say they are testing for the firefighter position. Well, our entry-level position is actually Firefighter / Engineer (each company has at least two Firefighter / Engineers who rotate driving and riding backwards), not Firefighter. By calling the position by the wrong name shows me that you have not done your homework.

Overview of the position / job description:

Make sure you know what the basic duties of the position are so you know what you are getting into and will be expected to do. If you are asked the question "Tell us about the duties of a firefighter for this agency," you can quote information from the job flyer (hopefully you also did more research such as stopping by fire stations and talking with the firefighters, visiting the web site, etc.). For those of you that are Paramedics, here is an important section. Many departments that provide ambulance service to their community expect the newly hired firefighters to work on the ambulance or keep their paramedic license for so many years. This is the section that might explain any such duties or expectations. Don't wait until after you're hired to say, "Nobody ever told me I was going to have to spend the majority of my time working on the box (ambulance)."

NOTE: I would always attempt to get a full job description for every position I was testing for. Many times, the job flyer only has an abbreviated version. Go to the Personnel / Human Resource office and ask them for a copy of the full job description. They are expected to have job descriptions for *EVERY* position in *EVERY* department, from the top to the bottom.

Overview of the department / community:

Many job flyers include basic information about the fire department and the communities served. Here is the start to your research that you can build upon. Many oral panels ask the question "Tell us what you know about the fire department and/or the community." Well, here is your starting point.

Minimum Qualifications (to take the test or remain employed after getting a job):

These items can vary from department to department. Some departments only require a candidate to be 18 years old and have a high school diploma or G.E.D. Others may require a candidate to be at least 21 years old, be a paramedic with at least two years of paramedic experience, and also have a state firefighter 1 certificate.

KEY POINT #1—Make sure you meet the minimum requirements or your application will usually be rejected. If you don't meet the minimum requirements, take note of what you do need to take that test in the future. Those are things you should be striving to obtain!

KEY POINT #2—If there are minimum qualifications to take the test, does the application state that you are to provide copies of those qualifications with your application? If so, follow those directions or your application may be rejected. I've heard too many candidates say they were rejected because they didn't include a copy of a certain certificate. Don't let yourself fall into the same trap—set yourself up for success by reading the job flyer and highlighting things such as what copies need to be included with the application.

Final Filing Date:

This is probably one of the most important things to note; highlight this date and time. I've heard too many candidates say, "I thought they were still accepting applications" after the filing period had ended. Note this date and put it in your calendar. You should actually turn that application in a.s.a.p. Some departments, actually use the date that the application was filed as a tie-breaker in case of a tie score on the hiring list. Why sit on it and take that chance? Also, some fire departments only pass out a certain amount of applications and accept a certain number back. I've seen filing dates as saying "Friday February 20 (or until 500 applications have been received—whichever comes first.").

A specific time frame that can range from one day to one month, where a department is accepting applications. A department may only accept a specific number of applications (first 25, first 50, first 100, first 500, etc.), or take any application that meets the minimum qualifications and is received by the final filing date.

Many fire departments only accept applications once every couple of years, some shorter, some longer. Because government hiring can depend on a number of factors, including budgets and available positions, there can be quite a variance in the way and frequency a department hires personnel. The key for you is to be on top of the game and find out about the tests before they open up, so you are well prepared. The best way to know that a fire department will be accepting applications would be to stay in contact with members of that fire department and personnel/human resources department. Additionally, subscribing to testing notification services will increase your chances of finding out about firefighter testing opportunities in a timely manner.

Application Screening Process:

Depending on the number of applications, some departments may prioritize applications based on qualifications. Some departments actually include desirable and highly desirable qualifications in their job flyer; if push comes to shove, this is an option for them to use to only have the most qualified candidates continue. If your application is accepted, the next phase will typically be the written examination.

Application Filing Location:

Some departments allow you to mail in your application, while some say you can drop them off in person at a certain location, on a certain date, and/or during a certain time frame. Some departments also only allow the person putting in the application to turn in the application. So before you have your friend or loved one drop it off (and have to face the rejection), read the fine print and follow the directions. I would always suggest going in person because you know it was received (unless it is an online submission).

Wages and Benefits:

You are usually not in the position to pick and choose between fire departments. If you are not already a full-time firefighter, there is virtually no reason why you shouldn't be taking every test you qualify for and then accept that first job offer. However, you still need to be aware of the wage and benefit differences between departments.

Some of the wage and benefit issues you should be aware of are as follows:

- **Salary**—I can't think of anyone that becomes a firefighter to get rich. Don't get me wrong, I believe I am well compensated for the work I do, and it allows me to lead a comfortable life. Regardless, you need to be aware of salary issues. Every now and then I hear candidates say that they wouldn't work for a certain department because they don't pay that well. If you don't have a job, are you really in a position to say that? I don't think so. Also, why are you becoming a firefighter—because you really want to do the job, or because you want to make great money? I know many firefighters that work at great departments for less money than they could make at not-so-great departments. To them, a great department might mean a high call volume or high fire volume.

  Salaries can be deceiving. Many departments start out their recruits at a little over minimum wage. One person told me they wouldn't work for this one big city because they only paid $2000 per month, and they couldn't afford that. I then asked if they had read the job flyer or done any homework. They said no. I told them to not believe everything they read. Yes, that department only pays you $2000 per month during the four-month recruit academy (many departments pay a lower wage during the academy because you really haven't proven yourself yet and because they can). Upon completion of the academy, that department then bumps you up to the range of $5000 per month (step 1 firefighter), and then once a year from that date you complete the academy, you are eligible to receive "step" raises to a top firefighter salary of around $7000 per month.

If you're not familiar with the term "step raise," it is a civil service term that most (if not all) fire departments use. Most departments have anywhere from five to seven steps. So, day one on the job (usually after the academy), you start at step 1, one year later you're at step 2, two years later at step 3, then finally four years later, you max out at fifth step. From there, the only way to get raises are to promote or if there are annual cost-of-living wages. Hopefully you see how that $2000 per month turns into $7000 per month within five or so years. Don't be deceived by what might just be academy pay or first year pay. If you are that concerned about salary, look at how much you top out and how long it takes you to get there.

- **Specialty pay:** In addition to the base salary, many departments pay extra money for any degrees you might possess (2 year, 4 year), certificates you might possess (EMT, Paramedic, Haz Mat Technician / Specialist), second languages you might speak, and so on. This extra pay can be up to 40% extra, on top of your salary. Do the math, it can truly add up. If the top step is only $5000, and you add 40% to that, you get an extra $2000 per month. Some departments pay a lower base salary (with a number of ways to receive specialty pay), while others pay a higher base salary (with very few ways to earn specialty pay). Either way, when you make a comparison, make sure you are comparing apples to apples.
- **Vacation leave:** All departments offer some form of paid vacation. Usually anywhere from a few shifts up to 15 or so shifts per year, depending on length of service.
- **Sick leave:** All departments offer some form of sick leave. Not that you should be planning on sick during your probationary year, you should be aware of the length of time available to you in case of illness or injury.
- **Holidays:** As a firefighter, you're going to work holidays. While you usually don't get overtime for working holidays, you do

usually receive some form of compensation such as extra time off or additional pay throughout the year.

- **Tuition reimbursement:** Many departments offer a form of program so you can attend training classes or complete your degree and receive all or partial reimbursement.
- **Medical Plans:** Most fire departments pay for an employee and their immediate family to be covered by medical insurance. Know the different plans available to you. Some cities don't actually pay for an employee's medical insurance. Instead they provide a higher base wage and deduct a certain dollar amount every paycheck based on the plan you choose. Why is this beneficial? Because if you have a spouse that has a better plan, then you might be able to get on their plan, and have that money you would have used, go towards your salary!
- **Retirement Plans:** Most fire departments do not participate in social security. Instead, they usually either offer a state or city administered retirement plan that allows you to retire after so many years of service, and receive a certain amount of money based on your total number of years of service. Many fire departments pay your retirement contribution, while others actually deduct the amount from your paycheck. Before you think that is bad, think again. The department I work for deducts my retirement contribution every check. To offset that payment, we are paid a slightly higher base wage than other similar local departments that have their department pay the retirement contribution. It allows me to retire out at a higher rate than if the department paid my retirement contribution. This is the same concept as if I paid my own medical benefits (as mentioned above). Most fire departments offer some form of retirement plan for its members. Most of the programs require a person to work until either they have reached a certain age or have obtained a minimum number of years of service (at which time they are vested). For example, in California, most fire departments utilize the Public Employees Retirement System (PERS) as their retirement plan. Even if you do not plan to

work in California or you get hired by a department utilizing a different retirement system, realize the concepts of this system are typical in most retirement systems.

How Does California PERS work?

There are two primary types of PERS retirement plans: one for "safety" members and one for "non-safety" or miscellaneous employees. Someone who is classified as a safety member is typically a sworn firefighter (or police officer); someone involved in fire suppression duties. While a fire chief is not usually involved in fire suppression duties, they still receive the safety retirement because that is what they started out receiving, assuming they came from the firefighter ranks at some point. A person receives the safety retirement, which provides a higher payout than the non-safety retirement, because of the hazards they are exposed to.

Regardless of the plan, the employee is usually expected to pay into their retirement, as is their employer. Retirement costs (like healthcare costs) are very expensive, and are something that comes into scrutiny by the public, especially since the average person today does not get anything even close, let alone a retirement plan at all.

You have to have at least five (5) years of service to be vested. That means you have to work at least five years to collect anything. Quitting with less than five years of service will force you to lose any monies that were contributed by you or for you by the department.

NOTE: The main thing to be concerned about regarding retirement plans is if you plan to leave a department for another. Make sure that other department has the same plan, because if it does not, you may not be able to transfer that service credit (and thus, work more years before you can retire in the new system). This is especially critical if you plan to move out of state, because there might not be any reciprocity. If you're planning on moving out of state, it is probably best to do it when you have very little time on the job (and won't be out too much if you lost anything) as opposed to when you are halfway through your career.

Testing Process:

Most job flyers give you an idea of what the testing process will consist of. Sometimes tentative dates are listed as well, so that you can plan ahead and make sure you are available (or do not plan anything else on that day, or plan to get the day off if needed).

KEY POINT—Do not believe everything you read. Almost anything can (and will happen).

I've heard candidates say that they didn't take a certain test because they were going to be out of town, or had some type of conflict with the tentative dates that were listed on the flyer. That is ridiculous. Are you 100% positive that they will keep that date? NO! Take the time to complete the application anyway. You might get lucky by them changing the date for some reason. If the dates then stay true to what was printed, then so be it. All you are really out is the time it took to fill out the application and the effort you made to get it. I would rather take that chance than miss out on a job opportunity because I believed what I read or what I heard.

The firefighter job flyer should not be looked at as an unimportant or useless batch of information. Take the time to read the ENTIRE job flyer and you can only benefit from the knowledge you obtain while doing so. Knowledge is power, and you never know when you might need to use it or show that you have it! Proper planning and preparation can only lead to one thing—success!

# # # #

CHAPTER 3

The Firefighter Job Application

One of the first steps of applying for a position with the fire department is to obtain and accurately complete the job application.

Applications can be obtained in a variety of ways:

- Downloaded from the fire department or city/county human resource/personnel website.
- In person from the fire department or city/county human resource/personnel department.
- From a friend or relative that went down to pick one up for you (be careful, read the job flyer carefully—some departments only pass out applications to the person that will be applying).

The job application is going to ask for specific information about yourself, your education, your experience, and about any certificates/ licenses you may hold specific to the position. While you think there may be a lot information asked for in the application, wait until you have to complete a background investigation. A background investigation packet is much more in depth, typically 20 pages or more, compared to a two to four page job application.

# # # #

Sample Firefighter Job Application:

APPLICATION FOR EMPLOYMENT

Acme Fire Department
4444 First Street - Anycity, CA 00000
Phone - (555) 555-5555 | Fax - (555) 555-1111

Position Applying For: _____   Date: _____

PERSONAL INFORMATION (*Please Print*)

Last Name:	First Name:		Full Middle Name:	
Mailing Address:	No. and Street:	City:	State:	Zip Code:
Home Phone:	Cellular Phone:	Other:	Email:	
Drivers License #:	State:	Class Of License (A, B, C):	Expiration Date:	

Have you ever been convicted of any offense by any civilian or military court?   Yes ___ No ___

If yes, explain. Give date and place of each offense; specific charge; date and place of conviction, and the fine or sentence received. You may omit any offenses for which the fine was less than $50. A criminal record is not necessarily a bar to employment. Each case is given individual consideration, based on job relatedness.

_____
_____

EDUCATIONAL & TRAINING HISTORY - *(Put an "X" in the box if you posses any of the following).*

	High School Diploma
	G.E.D.
	California High School Proficiency Certificate
	Emergency Medical Technician Certificate - If yes, expiration date: _____ Certifying Agency:

Name(s) and Location of College / University	Units Earned (*Semester or Quarter*)	Course of Study / Major	Degree Awarded and Year Degree Received

Certifications / Licenses: (Please list any applicable certifications or licenses not listed above)

_____
_____
_____
_____

EMPLOYMENT HISTORY

(Start with your present or last job and account for the past 10 years. Explain any gaps in employment history).

Current (or most recent) Position:

From: (Mo/Yr): To: (Mo/Yr):	Employer Name:	Your Title:	No. Of Employees You Supervised:
Hours Per Week:	Street or Mailing Address:	Your Supervisors Name:	
Base Salary / Wage:	City / State / Zip Code:	Supervisors Title:	Supervisors Phone #:
Reason For Leaving:	Duties:		

From: (Mo/Yr): To: (Mo/Yr):	Employer Name:	Your Title:	No. Of Employees You Supervised:
Hours Per Week:	Street or Mailing Address:	Your Supervisors Name:	
Base Salary / Wage:	City / State / Zip Code:	Supervisors Title:	Supervisors Phone #:
Reason For Leaving:	Duties:		

From: (Mo/Yr): To: (Mo/Yr):	Employer Name:	Your Title:	No. Of Employees You Supervised:
Hours Per Week:	Street or Mailing Address:	Your Supervisors Name:	
Base Salary / Wage:	City / State / Zip Code:	Supervisors Title:	Supervisors Phone #:
Reason For Leaving:	Duties:		

From: (Mo/Yr): To: (Mo/Yr):	Employer Name:	Your Title:	No. Of Employees You Supervised:
Hours Per Week:	Street or Mailing Address:	Your Supervisors Name:	
Base Salary / Wage:	City / State / Zip Code:	Supervisors Title:	Supervisors Phone #:
Reason For Leaving:	Duties:		

NOTE: If you need additional sections, please copy this page and list additional pages as page 2, page 3, etc.

May we contact the employers listed above? Yes ___ No ___ If no, indicate below which one(s) you do not wish us to contact: _____

Have you ever been terminated from employment within the last ten years?
Yes ____ No ____. If yes, please explain: _____
_____

I authorize employers and educational institutions identified in this employment application to release any information they have concerning my employment or education to the Acme Fire Department. Yes ____   No ____

CERTIFICATION STATEMENT

I understand employment may be offered after an evaluation of a background investigation, which will include employment history, references, criminal and motor vehicle records. I understand employment may be offered contingent upon an acceptable report from the Acme Fire Department's doctor after a pre-placement physical examination, which will include a drug screen. I understand that upon starting for work, I will be required to certify eligibility for employment under the guidelines of the Immigration Control Act of 1986 by completion of U.S. Department of Justice Form I-9. I further understand the Acme Fire Department does not guarantee employment for any specified period of time nor does it imply any eligibility for promotional opportunities with an offer of employment. I certify that the statements made by me in this application are true, complete, and correct to the best of my knowledge and belief, and are made in good faith. I understand and agree misstatements/omissions of material facts will cause forfeiture of my rights to employment by the Acme Fire Department and that I may be subject to termination if misstatements/omissions are discovered after employment beings.

_____   _____
Signature of Applicant: Date:

15 Tips To Successfully Complete
The Firefighter Job Application

You have been doing your research and looking for fire departments that are accepting applications for firefighter positions. You have found a department that is accepting applications. Here is your chance to get that badge you've been working so hard for. Probably the first impression that fire department will have of you is when you pick up and / or complete that application. Do not screw up a perfectly good chance (and easy way) at making a positive first impression! Obtaining and completing a job application for the position of firefighter should not be a situation that you take for granted or you do not take seriously. Unfortunately, some people do take it for granted and do not take it seriously. I've heard numerous candidates say "It's just another application," or "It's not that big of a deal," or "I've done numerous ones before, why should this be any different."

First of all, yes it is another application, but obviously something is not going right on your end and you have to fill another one out since you haven't got the job yet. Second, yes it is a big deal—it is for the job of your dreams! Lastly, if you're wondering why this application should be any different from the other ones you've completed, go back to the answer for my first quote. It should be different because maybe you are not properly completing the application or are making a not so stellar first impression.

Why do you need to put everything you have into every hiring process you go through? So you don't have to take another test!

My Basic Application Tips For Success:

You've done your research (either reactive or proactive) and you have found an opportunity to take a firefighter examination for a fire department. Pat yourself on the back (not too hard, you still need to make it through the entire process) for getting this far. Remember, this is an opportunity that might only come around once every three to five years (or longer depending on the department's situation). DON'T

WASTE A PERFECTLY GOOD OPPORTUNITY TO DO YOUR BEST! Here are what I consider to be 15 tips to successfully complete the firefighter job application:

Tip #1:
___

If you are required to pick up an application in person, always try to get an extra one or two. Why? If you screw up the first one, you have a second one to save the day. I can't count the amount of applications that I started to complete and I made a major mistake in some form or fashion and I would have been dead in the water if I didn't have a spare. Think about this for a second. You are busting your butt, doing everything you can do be a firefighter (I hope). When do you usually have time to complete the application? Probably late at night or some other non-opportunistic time where you are either tired or rushed for time. Some times, I know that getting a spare application is not feasible, since sometimes the department only hands out a limited number, or every candidate has to sign for each numbered application.

Also, you never know when a buddy might need one (don't make this a regular habit because people will come to expect you to always have one. Think of it as an insurance plan). You do someone else a favor (this is one of those major favors in life) and you never know when you might need them to do a favor such as this for you in the future. There are times when you can't pick up every application in person or you hear of a testing opportunity too late (all of your reactive and proactive methods obviously failed). Remember the old saying, "what you give is what you get."

Tip #2:
___

Complete the application either on your computer (if you are able to complete one over the internet) or a typewriter if you have access to one. Only hand-write applications if you have neat handwriting. I know typewriters are getting hard to find, but they can look nicer than handwriting if you have poor handwriting. If using a ballpoint pen, use a high quality pen of black or blue ink. Red is not a good choice because it may not copy well (some departments make copies of your application for the oral panel members). Whatever you do, don't use pencil!

One of my first firefighter tests was for the City of Stockton. I remember going to City Hall to pick up an application (yes, I grabbed two) and I saw this man sitting at the table in the personnel office filling out his application. That is not a bad thing in itself. What did not seem appropriate was his using pencil to complete the application. Pencil does not come across as professional, and also allows items to be erased (which can lead to problems later). Also, if you look at many applications, it specifically says "please type or print your application in blue or black ink." He failed the first part of the test, which was properly following directions.

Tip #3:

Have a copy of the job flyer in front of you. This is important because you want to ensure that you are qualified to take the test and that you follow all of the directions they request. It is almost impossible (and impractical) to list every certificate you may have obtained, but if one of those certificates is required or highly desirable, you want to make sure that you list it.

Tip #4:

Know all of your employment history that will be needed to complete the blanks in advance. How many of you know the exact details of every job you've ever held (salary, supervisors name, complete address, phone number, exact job titles, etc.)? If you don't, scrambling while you are filling out the application to get the information is not a good idea. Now is the time to find that information out.

Don't guess and just put anything or something close in there. That might get you disqualified during a background investigation or make you sound like an idiot when you're explaining to the background investigator "I wasn't sure, so I just estimated." That doesn't sound too professional or intelligent to me. Many job applications ask for information from either every employer you have ever had or for the last ten years.

For some of you, this isn't going to be easy. Planning in advance will save headaches and disappointment in the future. Even if they don't ask for it on the application, you can be assured they will during the background investigation. If you are not sure—don't estimate. Call that previous employer (hopefully you left on a good note) and someone in their personnel department might be able to help. The bottom line is that the information you provide better match up to what the employer will say about you—any discrepancy can lead to disqualification.

Tip #5:
_____

Know all of your <u>educational history</u> that will be needed to fill in the blanks. Many applications ask for information about each college you have ever attended (such as name and location, semester or quarter units completed, major, degrees received, and dates attended). Dust off those transcripts!

Tip #6:
_____

Do not leave any blanks! If the information requested does not apply to you, then put N/A on it (as opposed to leaving it blank). It shows you did not skip it.

Tip #7:
_____

Make sure that you check every box that is asking you information. Many times there are boxes with a yes or a no choice and it can be easy to skip over without checking one or the other.

Tip #8:
_____

Make sure you put the exact job title you are competing for on the job application. If you read the job flyer, you will find the exact job title.

I know it sounds basic, but I've seen a department test for Firefighter trainee, Firefighter (Lateral), and Firefighter/Paramedic all at the same time. Make sure you get considered for the appropriate position, and not disqualified because you don't meet the requirements of that "other" position.

Tip #9:

Don't include copies of every certificate you have ever received. If they ask for it, then include it. If they don't ask for them, don't include them. Otherwise, don't waste their time having to dig through non-essential information, while also proving that you cannot follow directions. About the only copies I have ever seen a department ask for during the application phase are EMT, Paramedic, Firefighter 1 academy, and Firefighter 1 certificate. The reason they are asking for those is to weed out the people that have the required certificates from those who don't, and also to get a pool of the "most qualified" candidates. Trust me, if you're lucky enough to get to the background investigation phase, they'll ask you for copies of everything at that point.

Tip #10:

Be honest. I know that should be an expected trait of every human being, but it is not. One lie or "stretching of the truth" can be enough to either eliminate you from the process or potentially terminate you from employment after you have received the job (most applications have that little clause in them just before you sign it that says something to that effect). Even if it is not an intentional lie or deception on your part, it can still backfire.

Say that you list you were employed from June 2010 through July 2012, but it was actually May 2010 through June 2012. I realize you're only off by a month in each direction, but put yourself in the shoes of the background investigator—what are they going to think? Even if you say, "It was a mistake," they are going to raise their eyebrows and wonder what else was just a mistake. Also, by saying it was a mistake;

you're making yourself look less than competent. It is your past and your history, if you don't know it, who else should? Don't chance it—it is not worth it!

Tip #11:
___

Stay away from using abbreviations except for accepted two-digit State abbreviations (like NY for New York), EMT, and maybe CPR. While you might know what they stand for, don't count on the person reviewing it to.

Tip #12:
___

If you put down a cellular number, make sure you actually answer it promptly. It amazes me when I call people and it takes them hours to return my call. I realize we're all very busy, but imagine you as the fire chief trying to call that candidate with a job offer. Do you think they are going to wait for you to return the call? How many others do they have to pick from on the list? While I'm on the subject, if you have a voice mail (home or cellular) recording, have you listened to it lately? Does it sound professional and mature?

I love it when I have students wanting fire information leave me a message with their cellular phone number to call them back on. When I return the call, it never fails. Sometimes I get the recording of "Yo, this is T's mobile phone (loud bass thumping in the background) and I'm not available . . . ." Would you want to hire this individual? Another great recording is when you hear a little two year old voice saying that you've reached the home of the Johnson's, Timmy, Margaret, Lisa, Jimmy, Bobbie, Fido, Kittie, etc.

While it might show you are a family oriented person, it doesn't present you in a positive, professional way. I returned a phone call the other day and introduced myself, said that I was from the college fire technology program, and that I was returning their call. He seemed angry that I was bothering him since he replied, "who?" Then of course his tone changed when I repeated myself. Be consistent, polite, and courteous—you never know who is going to be on the other end offering you a job (or thanking you for applying, and advising you to have a nice life).

Tip #13:

If you list an email address, make sure it is professional and appropriate. How are you going to convince an oral panel that you appreciate and understand diversity when you have an email address that is politically incorrect, sexually suggestive, or downright offensive? Remember who your audience is and that you are trying to convince the oral panel and fire department that you are mature, professional, and of the highest ethical standards. My suggestion is to have one with a first name (or initial) and last name. That is considered professional and appropriate.

Tip #14:

Do not fax your application in. Most departments don't allow you to anyway (faxes usually do not come out looking that good). If at all possible, drive it down and turn it in personally. Why? It gives you a chance to talk with the personnel employees and obtain information relating to the process (remember to make a good first impression, leave the Metallica shirt at home or under your jacket). It gives you the chance to see how long it takes to drive there (to make sure you properly plan your timetable for the testing process events. It gives you a chance to tour the city and perform some research, and the opportunity to stop by some fire stations and talk to some firefighters about the process.

Tip #15:

Last, but not least, make a copy of your application prior to turning it in. It will go into a file for that specific department which should include a copy of the resume you also turned in, and any information that you obtained during your research of the department. Number one this helps when you get called in for that interview many months after you turned it in so you know what you actually put on there (and can show them "look what I have done since then"). Number two; you never know when you might have to take that test again. Since this is a very competitive process, it is not uncommon for someone to have to take the same fire department exam at least once or twice in the years to follow. I took San Jose's test four times over the course of four years. Welcome to reality. Now if you have a file, you can just do "updated research."

A properly completed application can be the key to success; an improperly completed application can be a recipe for disaster. Take the time to do it right so you don't have to fill out another firefighter application again!

# # # #

Steve Prziborowski

Your Application Was Not Accepted?
Get Over It—And Move On!

A couple of years ago, a big-city fire department on the west coast was accepting 1,000 applications for the position of entry-level firefighter, over a one-day period, after having given out well over 1,000 applications earlier in the week. The job announcement stated only 1,000 applications would be accepted, and to specifically not line up prior to 5:00 am that morning the applications were being accepted. This was the first time in a number of years the city had reduced the entry-level requirements of either an EMT certificate or a Paramedic license to just 18 years of age and a high school diploma or G.E.D. The department was very up front in stating they needed to fill a little over 20 positions and they needed to get more "home grown" people to apply and hopefully get hired. The city, like many other big cities, was trying their best to increase the diversity of their fire department, to mirror the community demographics.

What seemed like a good plan from the administrative side easily turned ugly once people started lining up in advance, long before the 5:00 am time they were asked to do so. Candidates from around the state and I would imagine across the United States planned on camping out, for the sole purpose of trying to ensure their application was one of the first 1,000 applications accepted. Camping out is nothing new for submitting fire service applications. I remember when I started testing for the position of firefighter in the early 1990's; it was very common to camp out in line just to get an application or to submit an application. In those lines, you would typically find the "die-hard" candidates, the ones who were willing to do what it took to get a job as a firefighter. These were typically your candidates who were either working for other fire departments or were either current or former fire technology students from community colleges.

Well, what should have been a relatively problem free process immediately turned into a chaotic scene for a variety of reasons, resulting in a large number of unhappy candidates who had not been

42

able to submit an application. Local television news cameras were on scene filming the people camped out in line and even caught the fire chief and city staff members personally selecting people to submit their applications, and not in a first-come, first-serve manner. Allegations were flying that these people being hand selected were not "randomly selected," and were actually relatives of current fire personnel and city staffers, including one of the fire chief's sons. Apparently the process of randomly (or hand-picking as it appeared to be) selecting candidates did not bode well with virtually everyone involved, except of course to the 1,000 or so who were selected to continue.

In the following days, the Mayor agreed to have another day to allow those candidates who were not selected, to submit their applications. They would not give out additional applications; just accept any applications from candidates who had not made the cut that first day. For the most part, this appeared to appease those involved who had not been able to be one of the lucky first 1,000 applications. I had the chance to talk to a group of my students a few days after this situation; some who had been fortunate to submit an application, some who had not. It was interesting to hear the comments from the students who were all aspiring to become firefighters. Many of them were obviously angry and showing some disdain towards the city and the fire department because of what happened; however, they still wanted to work there. Comments from the students mimicked those comments found on various chat and discussion boards: the fire chief needs to be terminated; we need to sue the city; they passed over numerous candidates who were experienced, and already working for other fire departments; they were only selecting "unqualified" candidates; that they did not take the first 1,000 applications; that they had lowered their standards; to simply this is just B.S.

While I can feel the pain as I remember having to test for numerous fire departments, and go through somewhat similar processes (but not as chaotic as this one, which seems to win the prize for most chaotic) trying to get hired as a firefighter, I cannot help but think the following things when I hear such comments after having been employed as a firefighter for more than a few years now:

- Since when are anyone of us "entitled" to a job anywhere, let alone in the fire service? The last time I checked, the only thing we were entitled to was birth, paying taxes and death.

- Does terminating the fire chief solve the problem? Probably not. We have to remember who the fire chief works for—typically the city manager, the mayor, a city council, a board of directors, or some other form of government where they work as an "at will" employee—meaning they can get fired for any reason and they follow the direction of that governing board, regardless of whether they agree with the decisions made above their head and whether or not the decisions align with the wishes of the line firefighting personnel.

- Does suing the city solve the problem? Maybe in the short run, but remember the saying—you may have won the battle, but did you win the war? Probably not. I don't know about you, but I don't want to have gotten my job by suing the city just to get a chance at getting hired. When you typically work for a fire department for 20 to 40 years, something like this will be your reputation for your entire career, and even after you're retired. It will always be, "hey, remember that guy who sued the city just to get hired?" Sorry, but I'd rather be known for the more positive things I have accomplished in my career. I realize anybody can sue anybody for anything. But remember what happens if you win—where do you think the money to pay the lawyers and even pay you and anyone else comes from, should there be a monetary settlement? That money will probably come out of the city budget, which is meant to pay for staffing—wages and benefits, keep fire stations open, etc. Just because you get the chance to apply now, it doesn't mean you'll even get hired (do you think they want to hire the person that sued them? Come on; get real—would you want to hire someone that sued you?).

- Regarding the comment of passing over numerous candidates who were "more qualified" because they were working for other fire departments; remember that the job announcement did not mention they were looking for "lateral transfers" or other experience. An interesting comment in the newspaper was that many people were in line wearing their fire department uniforms. I don't know about you, but if I were testing for another fire department (even though I have no plans to do so), I wouldn't be wearing my fire department uniform. That just isn't cool, and doing so doesn't show much respect or loyalty to the department you're planning on leaving. Plus it may be against the rules or policies of your department to do so.

- As for the term "qualified", that is a very subjective term. What constitutes being the most qualified candidate? The best resume? The most degrees? The most years of experience? Fire experience versus no fire experience? The most certificates? See where I'm going? What one person thinks makes someone the best-qualified candidate may drastically differ from another person's opinion. A fire department does not hire a resume—they hire a person. Just because someone does not have every certificate or degree out there or does not have a lot of years (or any for that matter) of fire experience does not mean they will be a bad hire or even "unqualified." In reality, a fire department should be hiring for a positive, can-do attitude, and for what they think will be a "good fit" for their department, their culture, and their community. I know that seems subjective, but think back to 20 years or more, when there really wasn't a push for candidates to have EMT certificates, Paramedic licenses, and firefighter 1 certificates, etc. Think of the veteran firefighters currently on the job, those with 20 plus years on the job. Most of them did not have those certificates or degrees. Yes, they typically came with experience from the trades, but the key is that they were trainable.

- As for lowering standards, the last thing I think a department should do is lower a hiring standard. Instead, we should try to bring the level of candidates up to our standard, to ensure the standards are not lowered. However, in this case, the city knew if they wanted to attract home grown talent, they might have to not require the two common things they have required over the last few years—an EMT or Paramedic card. However, if I'm not mistaken, there was a stipulation that an EMT card was required by the start of the academy, so it wasn't like they were going to have to put the person through EMT school. At least they were up front in the news stories prior to the accepting of applications; they knew they needed diversity and if they required EMT or Paramedic cards to apply, they might be limiting their diversity pool to choose candidates from. Good, bad or indifferent, it is what it is and a city has an obligation to it's community to do it's best to reflect the demographics of that community.

- As for not taking the first 1,000 applications, if you read the job announcement, it stated they would accept 1,000 applications. I didn't notice that they would take the first 1,000—just 1,000. I realize that is vague and can be construed different ways, but if you read it carefully, they didn't violate what they said they would do.

- Regarding the process being B.S., welcome to reality. I'm not sticking up for what occurred, but no one fire department or city is perfect. There are always going to be mistakes made and unhappy people, especially when you limit the number of candidates. For anyone who works in public safety for more than a few years, you come to realize things are not always perfect and that there is always a better way to do something. Yes, maybe it was B.S., but what are you really going to do about it? It happened. Yes, you can be the one who is obviously frustrated and angry and bitter, but where is that going to get you in the long run? Nowhere, and your frustration, anger and bitterness will obviously show up at some point in the future, either during the hiring process or after you get hired (assuming you are fortunate enough to have that occur).

Could the process have been smoother and user-friendlier? Of course it could have been. However, we can Monday morning quarterback it forever and it still won't change what happened. I even heard of frustrated candidates making phone calls or sending emails to the fire chief, city staff, and others, expressing how mad they were, and how disappointed they were in the process. I realize a squeaky wheel usually gets the grease, but in this case, do you really want to be the one who is sticking out—in an annoying way? Don't get me wrong, I think we should stick up for what we feel is right. However, there is a right way and an appropriate way to do so, and it is also important to learn how to pick your battles.

The bright side is for those candidates who do still want to work there, and have some experience and qualifications they typically look for, you will have your opportunity at some point in the future. The positive thing about big city fire departments is that they typically test for firefighter pretty regularly. I truly think things are done for a reason, good or bad. If you didn't make the cut this time, it wasn't meant to be. However, that doesn't mean you won't have your chance in the future, and it may be the near future. I took the test for the department I work for twice over a couple of years, and I even took another big city test a few times over a couple of years, so it is not uncommon to get a second chance within a year or two to take the test for that same department, before getting hired as a firefighter.

What I ask of you if you were a part of this process, heard about this process, or ever has such a process occur to you—either in your pursuit of becoming a firefighter or after getting hired, you really need to think whether it is worth getting emotionally charged and attached to what has transpired. More times than not, we act based on emotion as opposed to rationality, and that can get us into trouble, making us say or do things we will regret later on. I have nothing but respect for the fire department in question and their personnel; I personally know and respect many members of various ranks. What occurred was unfortunate, and the damage is probably done. But if nothing else, it is hopefully a learning experience for all of us—whether we work there or aspire to work there or anywhere as a firefighter for that matter.

Lastly, I hate to be blunt, but we need to remember that it is not a right that we are hired by a fire department—it is a privilege. Unfortunately some folks think they are entitled to do certain things in life, such as submitting applications. There is a fire department out there for everyone, as long as you don't give up and keep on testing. Maybe this fire department was not for you, as difficult as that may be to swallow. Or, maybe it was. If you truly think it is the department for you, you'll take their test again and try to not get caught up in the current emotions, as it will make you look very negatively. Would you like to hire someone who is negative, especially about the department they are applying for?

# # # #

Supplemental Questionnaires

In addition to the regular job application, some fire departments also have a supplemental questionnaire, to help further decide whether you are worth continuing in the hiring process and to determine if you have specific qualifications they are looking for. Most cities and counties use a standard job application for every position within the city or county. These standard job applications are relevant for firefighters, police officers, dogcatchers, and just about any position that might be classified within their civil service system. However, since each division within a city is slightly different (with different knowledge, skills, and abilities requirements), some positions will also have the candidate complete a supplemental questionnaire.

The reason I've included these sample questionnaires is so you can prepare for possible questions you may be asked. If you look at the questions below, you'll see they are all oral board interview questions being asked as a written assignment. Before answering questions like these, ensure you are up-to-date with how to answer oral board questions. More information on how to answer oral board questions can be found in later sections of this book.

Supplemental Questionnaire for Firefighter—Sample #1:

The purpose of this questionnaire is for you to identify your qualifications and experience in job related areas. A panel will review applications and supplemental questionnaires of candidates who meet the minimum requirements and select the best qualified candidates. Although you may possess the minimum requirements for this examination, you are not guaranteed advancement in the process. It is critical that you fill out the supplemental questionnaire completely, listing all education, experience, or special training, which might demonstrate your qualifications.

Please type or print your responses on 8 ½" x 11" paper. Attach this cover sheet, and put your name at the top of each page. Your answers should be concise, complete and clear. Grammar, clarity of expression, and legibility will be considered in the evaluation process

- Please describe why you are interested in a career with our fire department.
- What qualifications do you possess that has you prepared for this position?
- What do you see as the most satisfying aspect of being a firefighter, and what do you see as the most dissatisfying aspect of being a firefighter?
- As a firefighter for our department, it is important that you establish and maintain effective working relationships. Describe how you would handle diverse personalities or differences in opinion with other members of your team.
- What is the public expectation of firefighters in the community at times other than emergencies?
- In addition to the above questions, if you are applying for a paramedic position, please answer the following:
- Our fire department prides itself in offering superior customer service and patient care. What personal attributes and experience do you possess that will ensure you provide the highest level of patient care possible for our communities served?
- Provide a chronological description of your paramedic training and licensure process, including the following: schools attended, internship location and description, National Registry Exam dates, State license status.
- Briefly explain your work experience as a paramedic.

Supplemental Questionnaire for Firefighter—Sample #2:

Responses to the following supplemental questions must be submitted with your application:

- Please describe how your work history has prepared you for this position.

- Briefly outline your educational background and any special certifications you have that relate to the position of firefighter.
- Explain any special skills that you have that would assist you in your career as a firefighter.
- Our fire department is a progressive, team-oriented organization, which places great emphasis on customer service, public education and fire prevention. Describe how you have demonstrated the ability to work as a team member and what character traits you will bring to our organization.

Supplemental Questionnaire for Firefighter—Sample #3:

The City takes pride in the honesty and integrity of their employees and in the high level of service that they are able to offer the citizens in our City. Maintaining this excellence is an important goal of the department when looking for new employees. In keeping with this tradition of pride and excellence, please assist us by answering the questions applicable to the position you are applying for and return it with your application.

Please provide a brief explanation on the back of this page for any question marked YES. Note: A yes answer does not necessarily mean you will be excluded from the process. Each item is taken on a case-by-case basis.

1. Have you used illegal drugs in the past four years?
2. Have you ever been convicted of a felony?
3. Have you been convicted of a serious theft as an adult?
4. Have you had any driving related convictions in the last three years?
5. Are you willing to communicate with members of the public who may be angry or upset and directing that emotion on you?
6. Are you willing to work with people of varying ethnicities, backgrounds and education levels?
7. Are you willing to work at a job where your assignment may be suddenly changed to meet the needs of the Department?

8. Have you ever been involved in or conspired to commit arson?
9. Have you ever committed or conspired to commit insurance fraud?
10. Are you willing to work different shifts, holidays and weekends?

I have carefully read and responded honestly to all of the questions listed under the position I am applying for. I am also aware that this questionnaire will be used during the examination process in determining my suitability for a position with the City, and that all of my answers will be verified as part of the hiring process which will include a polygraph exam. If employed, I understand that any falsification of this record may be considered cause for disqualification or termination from employment.

Supplemental Questionnaire for Firefighter—Sample #4:

The completion of this supplemental questionnaire is required for your application to be considered for the Firefighter position, and is an integral part of the examination process.

This supplemental questionnaire will be used to assess your experience as it relates to the position of Firefighter. Your responses will be evaluated and will assist in determining which applicants will receive further consideration in the exam process.

Please respond to each of the following questions. Place your full name and the position you are applying for at the top of the page. Include the name of your employer, your job title, and the dates you performed the described experience in your response to each question. If you apply online, you will have space to insert your answers and will not need to attach a separate copy.

1. EMT/Paramedic Status (Check all that apply):
    a. Currently have a National Registry EMT certificate and have attached my certificate to application.
    b. Currently have a valid California EMT certificate and have attached my certificate to my application.

    c. I am in process of obtaining my EMT certificate and will have it by _____.

    d. Currently CPR certified and have attached my certificates to my application.

    e. I am in process of obtaining my CPR certification and will have it by _____.

    f. Currently certified as a California Paramedic with current certifications in Advanced Cardiac Life Support (ACLS), Pediatric Advanced Life Support (PALS or PEPP), and Pre-Hospital Trauma Life Support (PHTLS) or Basic Trauma Life Support (BTLS), or equivalent and have attached my license and certificates to my application.

    g. I am in process of obtaining my Paramedic license and required certifications and will have them by

    _____.

    h. None of the above.

2. Submission of a valid CPAT card is required at time of application. Cards must be dated after May 1 of last year.

    a. I have a current CPAT card and have attached a copy of my card.

    b. I have registered at http://www.cpatonline.org and am scheduled to take the physical agility exam. I understand my application will be considered incomplete until I take the test and therefore may not be included in the first 250 qualified applications.

    c. I have not yet registered.

3. Please check current certifications you possess:

    a. CPR

    b. ACLS

    c. PHTLS

    d. BTLS

    e. ITLS

    f. PEPP

    g. PALS

4. What firefighting certificates do you possess?
    a. Firefighter 1 Academy completion (from a community college)
    b. California State Fire Marshal Firefighter I
    c. California State Fire Marshal Firefighter II
    d. California State Fire Marshal Rapid Intervention Team
    e. California State Fire Marshal Confined Space Operations
    f. California State Fire Marshal Prevention 1
    g. California State Fire Marshal Vehicle Extrication
    h. California State Fire Marshal Rescue Systems 1
    i. California State Fire Marshal Trench Rescue
    j. California Specialized Training Institute (CSTI) or California State Fire Marshal Haz Mat First Responder Operational Level
    k. ICS 100, 200, 700, 800
    l. National Wildfire Coordinating Group (NWCG) or California State Fire Marshal S-130 and S-190

5. Please check all that apply:
    a. I have volunteered for a fire department.
    b. I am currently working as a volunteer firefighter.
    c. I am currently working as a paid firefighter.
    d. I have gone through a junior firefighter or explorer firefighter program.
    e. I have prior firefighter vocational training or work experience.
    f. None of the above.

6. You are required to take and receive a passing written test score through National Testing Network by May 3 of this year. The test must be dated after May 15 of last year.
    a. I have taken the Fire test through National Testing Network and have directed that my scores be submitted to this fire department.

b. I will register at http://www.nationaltestingnetwork.
    com and schedule myself to take the test before May 3
    of this year.

c. I do not intend to take the test.

# # # #

CHAPTER 4

Resume Preparation

Creating the perfect resume that brings out the best in you, as well as showcasing your knowledge, skills, and abilities, is not that difficult (at least it should not be that difficult!). In most of the college level fire technology classes that I teach, I require the students to turn in a resume. I'm not necessarily telling them what is right and what is wrong; I'm suggesting ideas and changes based on my experience and opinion. Of the resumes that I see, the majority of them are <u>boring</u> and do not make a very good first impression. Many of them also have at least one spelling error. Your resume should be easy to read, straight forward, to the point, and present you as the most qualified candidate for the position you are applying for.

Frequently Asked Questions (FAQ) Regarding Resumes:

1. **What is a resume?**

   It is a brief (one-page or less) "snapshot" of you and your qualifications for the position you are applying for; nothing less, nothing more. What they should put on a resume and what they should not put on a resume confuses some people. To start off with we need to clarify something. A resume is **NOT** a job application. Many people think those words are synonymous with each other. They are not.

2. **What are the differences between a
resume and a job application?**

A job application usually asks for everything (you usually
don't have a choice of what to put in the boxes because you are
specifically requested to provide certain information) whereas a
resume is left up to you to decide what goes on the paper, and
in what order.

A job application can be anywhere from one page up to six
pages, whereas your resume should not be more than one page.
Not every employer is going to request or even allow you to
provide a resume, whereas most (if not all) are going to require
you to fill out some type of job application.

3. **Why do we need a resume?**

Some agencies might actually require you to provide one
with your application. If they do not specifically ask for one,
then you should always attempt to provide them with one at the
time you are turning in an application. Some agencies might
use the resume as a screening tool, to narrow the applicant pool
down to a more manageable number of candidates; especially if
they want to only have candidates with specific qualifications
or certifications continue in the process.

4. **Do all agencies allow resumes?**

When I was testing to become a firefighter, most agencies
allowed resumes to be turned in when the application was filed.
I have rarely seen applications that stated "no resumes will be
accepted." While many agencies allow resumes at the time of
application, some do not accept them after that point because
of the sheer volume of candidates and paperwork that is added
to the process.

5. **What about an updated resume at the time of my oral interview?**

While most agencies allow resumes to be accompanied with the job application, many of those agencies do not allow you to provide an updated resume at the time of your oral interview. That is why it is so important to turn one in at the time you submit your application—you might not have that second chance to submit one at your oral interview.

The only reason you should turn in an updated resume at the time of your oral interview would be if you have some changes that have occurred since the time you originally submitted your first resume. In the past, I remember turning in my initial application and then not having my oral interview until six months to three years after the initial application was filed! Now, hopefully you can see the benefit of offering to submit an updated resume at the time of your oral interview.

When they ask you "why do you want to provide a resume, we already have the one you submitted with your application?"—you can tell them that you have added various certifications, degrees, accomplishments, etc. to that initial resume and you want them to be aware of how far you've gone from that point to today.

6. **What do I need to list on a resume?**

I believe in short and sweet. I believe in using <u>major headings</u> such as objective, experience, education, community service / volunteer work, certificates / licenses, special skills, etc. You don't need to use all of them—just what you need (and what you have to offer in the way of knowledge, skills, and abilities). Pages 70 through 75 of this book will cover what information should be contained in each of those major headings.

7. **Should I pay someone to do put together my resume?**

Not unless you have extra money you don't mind parting with. If you can use a computer, and are familiar with Microsoft Word, then you should be able to do just fine. Microsoft Word has numerous resume templates in their office software that you can just type in your information and it produces a nice quality resume. I just do it the old fashioned way. I take a blank Word document and start typing away. When I first started testing, I did not have a computer (yes, computers had already been invented and becoming a common site in many households—I'm not that old), so I had to have a friend of mine type one up for me.

Initially that wasn't a problem. Unfortunately, it got to be a pain (more for him I imagine) to have to go over to his house and have him change the objective because I was taking another test, or even just to add a certificate. It was one of the reasons that forced me to buy a computer and also improve my basic computer skills. Why should you trust someone else to do something so important (and critical to your success) that you can easily do yourself? If nothing else, it provides you with more experience in computer usage, which will be another valuable skill to sell during your interview. Even as a firefighter, you should have a basic understanding of computer usage.

8. **If I type up my resume on a computer, how do I print out the copies?**

Unless you have a high quality laser printer at home, I would suggest going down to your local copy shop to print out your resumes. They usually sell high quality resume paper, and have high quality printers. Using lower quality printers can leave your resume looking less than desirable. If you use your computer to create the resume, just save it on a portable format (flash drive, etc.) and take that to the copy shop and use their computer to print it your resume.

9. **What color and quality resume paper should I use?**

You can't go wrong by using white, beige, or gray. I would stick to using conservative colors (as opposed to flashy and bright colors). If you were going for an advertising or marketing job that required you to be creative or catchy, then by all means use that neon orange paper. Otherwise, remember that the fire service is still predominantly very conservative. Stick to conservative paper. Also, make sure it is good quality paper and not flimsy like normal copy paper. Good copy shops have racks of quality resume paper to choose from.

10. **How many pages should my resume be?**

I am a firm believer in keeping a resume to <u>one page</u>, unless you are going for a chief officer position. When I interviewed for my Captain's position, I used a one-page format. While I had enough information to fill two pages, I still felt the necessity to keep it at one page. Why? Because one page is simple, easy to follow, and forces you to "cut to the chase." Too many resumes are extremely wordy and hard to follow. Using one-page forces you to keep only the relevant and important information about you.

11. **I am listing my experience on my resume, what should be the first item under the experience heading?**

The common way to list experience is to use the chronological method. That means your present job is listed first and then you work backwards, going down the page.

12. Do I need to list every job I have ever held on the resume?

Remember how an application differs from a resume. On the application, you are forced to include every job. The resume allows you to put only those jobs you feel necessary or relevant to the position you are currently going for. At the bare minimum, you should always list a present job (assuming you have one). If you have worked at numerous jobs in your lifetime, I would stick to having no more than three or four jobs on a resume. That way you leave space for other important items such as education or community service.

13. Do I need to list every certificate I have ever received on the resume?

Please don't bore the panel with all of your certificates. Stick to the major selling points (EMT, Paramedic, Firefighter 1 Academy, Firefighter 1 Certificate, etc.). That shouldn't mean you should stop preparing yourself by not taking any more certified classes once you get the above listed certificates, it just means you might not have time or space to discuss all of them.

14. How often should I be updating my resume?

I am a firm believer in the belief that if you are not updating (adding) to your resume at least once every two months, you are probably not doing as much as you probably should be doing in the way of preparing yourself for the position (entry-level or promotional). You should be always looking at ways to add items such as new certificates, educational accomplishments, professional accomplishments, and/or volunteer accomplishments.

Think about it this way. You turn your application and resume in today. It will probably be anywhere from two months to six months (or even a few years depending on how long the list will remain active) before you even get that first interview. If you have been adding accomplishments to your resume, here is a perfect way to present that updated resume to your oral interview panel.

Many times, when you try to provide a resume during the oral interview, they will usually tell you that they already have a copy of one that was provided by the Human Resources / Personnel Department. At that point, you can advise them that you understand that, but that you have also added some educational accomplishments, certificates (whatever) since the time you first filed the original application and resume. You then let them know that you wanted to make sure the board had the most up-to-date information about how much you are preparing yourself to become a firefighter.

If I were on the panel, I would be very impressed if I saw a great deal of improvement since the first resume. A good majority of the candidates do not either bother to update their resume or have not been doing as much as they probably should be doing in the way of preparation and motivation.

Creating the perfect resume should not have to be a major ordeal. If you stay on top of your resume, always keeping it updated, and always looking at other people's resumes (to see if you can learn something good or bad in relation to how they have packaged their resume), you should find yourself to be successful and have more time to worry about other things such as better preparing yourself for the job or taking time out for fun, family, and friends!

# # # #

15 Tips To Create A Better Resume

Your impression starts the minute the oral board encounters something related to you. One of the key things you can do to be able to make a positive impression is to have a powerful, attention-grabbing resume that is short, easy to read, and straight to the point.

Many of us probably cringe at the thought of having to provide a resume, or update a resume for an upcoming interview or application process. Producing and keeping your resume updated don't have to be that difficult or stressful. A properly prepared resume can distinguish you from other candidates as well as showcase the knowledge, skills, and abilities that make you the best fit for the position.

Tip #1: Keep it to one (1) page.

Unless you are competing for a chief officer position (and you have over 10 years of specific experience to the field you're applying for) you don't have that much that can't be squeezed onto one page. If it can't fit on one page, it probably isn't important enough or relevant enough to be on there. When I took my Captain's oral interview, I had a one-page resume. It was tough to squeeze everything on there (and have to leave things out), but I made it work. I received a 100% score on my oral interview, so I guess a one-page resume didn't hurt me.

Tip #2: 12-point font size is suggested for text.

I've seen ones that are in 9-point and 10-point font (as well as 18-point font). 12-point font size is standard for text—anything smaller and people are going to strain their eyes, anything larger is going to be obnoxious. Usually the people reviewing your resume are not just fresh out of college. They usually have some experience behind their belts and with experience comes declining eye site. How are you going to keep someone's attention if they have to strain to read your writing?

Tip #3: Keep it short, sweet, to the point, and leave plenty of open space to distinguish between things you want to stand out.

If you're writing more than two to three lines of text in a row, it is going to read like a paragraph. People reviewing resumes usually don't have time to read novels—they want one to two lines that are separated by open space, maybe accented with bullets or other objects, and pleasing to the eyes. Think about if you hand out an updated resume when you walk into the room. If you write paragraphs, there is the tendency they will not see key points (because all the words blend together after a while) and that they will miss things. Even if they had the time to review the one you turned in with your application, they usually don't have more than a minute or two to read it—that is why it is important to be short and sweet, making things stick out and be noticeable.

Tip #4: Make sure you keep it from being BORING.

Many resumes are plain, difficult to read, and will put the reader to sleep. Use type sets such as uppercase, sentence case, bold, underline, italics, in addition to just the plain old regular computer print. Alternating type sets will help the reader distinguish and pick out certain things about you and what you have to offer, while also ensuring that certain things about you are highlighted.

Tip #5: Update it regularly.

If you're not updating your resume at least once a month, you're probably not doing as much as you can to prepare yourself to become a firefighter. Updates can include additional education or training, another relevant certificate, more hours of community service / volunteer time, etc.

Tip #6: Bring sufficient copies to an interview.

If you are going to bring a resume to the interview (updated resume or initial resume), I would suggest bringing at least seven (7) resumes with you. I had an entry-level interview once with seven oral board members. Talk about intimidating. Most oral boards usually only have three to five members on them, but how would you feel if you only had five resumes and there were six people in front of you? What are you going to do now? Only pass out five of them and leave one person in the cold? How do you think that person is going to score you? I bet you would be embarrassed and it would potentially make you so nervous that you screwed up that you would not do as well as you should.

Tip #7: Do not list: "References available upon request."

It is a waste of space and I've never had any department ask me for references at the time of application or while you're going through the entry-level process. If they want references, they'll usually ask you as a part of your background investigation paperwork. It might work in the business world, but to me it is one line of text that can be used more wisely.

Tip #8: Stick to neutral colors—white, gray, beige, etc.

If you want to stand out, having bright colored resume paper is probably not the best way.

Tip #9: Don't forget to list your name, address and phone number.

A few years ago, we were looking at hiring some new EMT instructors at the college. One excellent candidate turned in his resume (no job application, just a resume as a screening tool). However, when I made an attempt to find a way to contact him to bring him in for an interview, I couldn't locate an address or a phone number. He had just put his name on the top of the resume and went into his qualifications.

The scary part is that he was already a Captain at his fire department. The only thing I can assume is that he used the same resume that he used for his Captain's promotional exam (even then that is risky because it bucks the normal trend). That is fine for his fire department because I think they knew how to contact him, but it was not acceptable to me because I did not have a way to contact him. He failed at making a positive first impression. Learn from his mistake.

Tip #10: Try to stay away from using abbreviations on your resume.

About the only acceptable abbreviations are EMT, CPR, or the State you live in. Why is that? Well what might be an abbreviation of one word might be the abbreviation of another word to someone else. In the medical field, PE can stand for patient exam, pulmonary edema, or pulmonary embolus. Not that you're probably going to list PE on your resume, but I think you get the point.

Think about who might read your resume—it might not just be a fire service professional. Folks from the Human Resources / Personnel department might be the ones reading it (or screening it) first or during an oral interview, and you can't expect them to know fire service abbreviations. Also, many departments have a citizen from the community on the oral panel. Do you think you're going to score points if you're talking about things they are not aware of? Also, writing out words can be perceived as being more professional or mature.

Tip #11: The only name, street address (2544 Jones Street), zip code, and phone numbers that should be on your resume should be your own!

Do not list names of references (I've seen that done) or names of supervisors. You know my opinion on listing references. As for names of supervisors, that information will be going on the application. Another problem with listing names on your resume is that not everyone you list is going to be well liked. I realize the oral board is supposed to be objective—not subjective. However, if you list the name of a reference on there that might not be a "quality reference" in the eyes of the evaluator (oh yes, it is a very small world); you put yourself at risk of getting the maximum points. I know that subjectivity is not supposed to occur in the oral board process, but it is almost impossible to eliminate bias and personal opinions in the testing process.

Tip #12: Be careful with the email address you list.

If you're going to list email addresses on your resume, avoid ones such as or OaklandRaidersRule@whatever.com—Oh yes, I've seen many similar ones. I am not here to judge folks on their hobbies, personal lives, or professional sports team choices. I am just offering the suggestion that you might want a more "professional sounding" one such as your first and last name. I know we're supposed to be objective, but put yourself in the shoes of a fire chief reviewing resumes of candidates they plan to hire as firefighters for the next 30 years, representing their community and their department. Just like cars and the clothes we wear can be an extension of our personalities and attitudes, so can email addresses.

I have no problem with the Oakland Raiders. But what if the person reading your resume is a 49'er fan and hates the Raiders? Or what if you are a female on the oral panel reviewing resumes and you see a LadiesMan@yobaby.com—I know we're not supposed to be biased, but can you blame them if they are? Also, for those of you with aol.com email accounts: if you have a "member profile," I would suggest reviewing it to make sure you would not be ashamed if a fire chief that was looking to hire you saw that profile. I make the EMT students at the college provide a resume to me and every now and then, I go check to see if they have a member profile, and there are always a few students that list things that would probably be found to be "unprofessional."

Tip #13: Don't list hobbies on your resume.

You're not getting hired for your hobbies—you're getting hired for your knowledge, skills, and abilities (in addition to how well you perform throughout the testing process). Nothing says you can't talk about them during the interview, go ahead. To me it is a waste of space on your resume. Also, what might be a "cool" hobby to you (snowboarding, bungee-jumping, motorcycling, jet skiing, etc.) might not be so "cool" to the Chief Officer reviewing your resume.

Getting back to subjectivity—every fire department has probably experienced folks getting injured off-duty doing some of those "cool" things. The last thing we need is another injury that is just waiting to happen. Chief Officers are usually trained or educated in risk management concepts. Let me see, this candidate likes to jump from planes, race fast vehicles, etc . . . If they take risks off duty, they might do them on duty . . . . Don't let people's minds wander—they will go places you don't want them to go.

Tip #14: Have somebody else take a look at your resume to proofread it for errors or things that just don't make sense.

Remember when you've been staring at your "masterpiece" for a while, changing things, adding things, etc., you are going to get tunnel vision and after a while, you wouldn't even be able to realize you had misspelled your name. Trust me, been there, done that, got the t-shirt. One misspelled word can be enough to have the person reading it convinced that you don't care about the way you present yourself.

Tip #15: Last, but not least, make a copy of every resume you ever turn in.

You should be making a copy of everything you turn in to a department (application, resume, etc.) and keeping it in a file. Other relevant items to keep are the initial job flyer and any information you obtained in the process. Keeping a copy of your resume can jog your memory when you get that interview four years later (I was actually called by a department I had tested with four years prior, to see if I wanted to be considered for employment). I didn't go to the interview because I had already been hired in a "dream department." Imagine if I had gone to that interview and they had asked me "What have you done since the time you turned in the original application?" If I hadn't kept a copy of the application, I would have looked pretty stupid. If I had kept copies, I could have been able to say with confidence "Look what I have done since then," to show my motivation and drive towards becoming a firefighter.

SUMMARY:

That is about all I have to offer in regards to producing the best resume you can. Use what you feel might benefit you. That first 30 seconds or so when you walk through the door to greet the oral interview panel are some of the most valuable seconds you will ever have to make a first impression. Already having produced a quality resume prior to the interview (and having turned it in with your application) will help set the stage for your entrance into the room since the interview panel usually reviews your application and resume prior to interviewing you. It will also start you out on a good note, thus leaving a positive first impression. Even if you turn in your first resume at the time of oral interview when you walk in the door, or you provide an updated resume at this time, it is still counted as part of your "first impression time."

The bottom line is that you always need to have a resume ready to go at any given time. Keep it on your computer (backed up in a different location) so that you can change the objective for every test you take, and be able to easily add the achievements you have accomplished since the last time you updated the resume.

JUST REMEMBER—YOU DON'T GET A SECOND CHANCE TO MAKE A FIRST IMPRESSION!

# # # #

Basic Information That Should Be On Your Resume

Your resume is a "snapshot" of you, your qualifications, and your knowledge, skills, and abilities. The purpose of a resume is to give a "down and dirty" quick look at your background to see if it relates to the position you are being considered for. Putting too much information on a resume is almost as bad as putting not enough information on a resume.

Can you honestly say that your resume is a masterpiece? Not too many people can. Most resumes that I see are drab, boring, blah, and either full of useless information or inadequate information. Whoever is reading your resume might have less than a minute to do so. Do you believe you make an awesome impression of yourself with your resume in less than a minute? Remember that the person that is reading your resume has probably seen numerous other resumes over the course of the day, the week, the course of the interview process for a specific hiring process, and over the course of their life. The point I'm trying to make is that your resume must be able to promote all of your knowledge, skills, and abilities in a positive, unique and refreshing way that is different from all of the other candidates.

Major Headings (Sections) Of A Resume:

I believe there should be no more than about five (5) major headings or sections contained in your resume, depending on what you have to offer. Some of the major headings I believe in are your objective, experience, education, community service / volunteer service, certificates / licenses, and/or special skills and training. Let me discuss each section in detail:

Objective:

A one-line description of what position you're going for and with what agency. Some people say you don't need an objective. I disagree. By listing the exact job title (taken from the job description) and the agency you're testing for, I think it shows a little effort and personalization.

Listing no objective is almost as bad as listing something like "to become a firefighter (and nothing else)." That makes it look like you use the same resume for every department. A little effort can go a long way. Also, stay away from objectives that are three to four lines long that sound like a story with no obvious ending. I've seen ones that say something to the tune of "to obtain a position that will allow me to utilize my knowledge, skills, and abilities to be able to serve the community, and so on, and so on, and so on . . . ." Get to the point! *To become a Firefighter for the Alameda County Fire Department* gets your point across perfectly.

Experience:

Some people like to write employment history or job history or work experience. I like experience because it is short and sweet, and because it can be paid or volunteer experience. List two to three employers at the most (don't stress—the rest are going on the application since most applications require you to list EVERY employer you have ever worked for). Start with your present employer and work backwards (chronological order), not leaving any obvious gaps.

For each employer, I like the following information:

- **Name of Employer** (Company—not the name of your supervisor)
- **City and State of employer** (no street address, no zip code, no phone number)
- **Exact Job Title**—this is the title the background investigator is going to verify you held when you worked there.
- **Dates Employed**—all you need is the month and date. The exact date will go on the application. June 2002 or 06/02 is sufficient. Just like your job title, make sure your dates employed match what the personnel department at your employer (or ex-employer) has on record for you. If they don't match up—that will bring up a red flag. Say you list that you started in June and your employer says you started in May. Put yourself in the shoes of a background investigator. It either gives the impression that

71

you are lying about something, or that you are not responsible at keeping records on your personal life.

- **Duties / Responsibilities**—Here is a section I can actually justify <u>not</u> listing on a resume. Why? Because you have already listed them on your application and because they can take up needed space for other things. I've seen resumes where the experience section took up ¾ of the page. Don't get me wrong— experience is one of the best things we can offer. However, experience itself is not everything. You have to balance it with education and other knowledge, skills, and abilities. If you need words on a resume—keep the duties / responsibilities. If you need to save space, eliminate them.

Education:

This section should be no more than a couple of lines. List any degrees you may possess. You only need to list one or two schools (one to two lines per school). Keep it simple. List the name of the college, the city and state of the college, your degree you received or are pursuing, and your date of graduation or expected date of application. That's it. If you graduated from college over 10 years ago, you might want to leave that date off of the resume (it will still usually be required on the application)—just to eliminate any potential bias based on age.

Some people ask me "should I list my units received, or all five of the colleges I've been to—including the ones I went to but never completed my degree?" NO! Remember—all of that information is usually requested on the application (it usually says "List every school you have ever attended.") and the resume is left up to you to *PICK AND CHOOSE* what goes on it.

Last, but not least—do not list your high school information! Why? First of all, that information will be going on the application. Second, it can show your age (which can be negative or positive). Even though it is illegal to discriminate based on age, it can potentially happen. If I'm on the oral panel and I think you are very immature, don't add fuel to the fire by showing that you just graduated last month from high school. I'm supposed to evaluate you on the answers you provide to the questions; however, if you add things in there such as high school dates, it can potentially go against you. Third, it is a waste of space! Chances are you are in college now or taking college-level classes (EMT, Firefighter 1 Academy, etc.), so it is unnecessary!

Community Service / Volunteer Service:

You are performing volunteer work, aren't you? Many fire departments almost expect their candidates to have some experience in volunteer or community service work. When I say community service, I don't mean the type where you put on an orange vest to do the weekend roadside cleanup work after getting convicted of a crime (not that there is anything wrong with that . . . .). I like to list volunteer work like my experience. List the name of the organization, city and state, what exact title you have, maybe some brief duties (if you have room), and most importantly, a running tally of your total amount of volunteer hours you have performed.

Janet Jackson performed the song "what have you done for me lately?" Think of volunteer service this way. Putting down that you helped out at a neighborhood cleanup day for two hours yesterday is not bad. However, as the months progress, if that is the only thing you have on your resume, it doesn't look to good. That was then, this is now. That is why I suggest picking something that you can continuously do over time (and wouldn't mind continue doing even after getting hired as a firefighter). That way you can show continuity, just like staying at the same job for a period of time can show loyalty, dependability and stability.

Many people tell me "I'm so busy that I don't have time to volunteer." Who does? I bet you can find something you can do to better the lives of someone or something else, even if it is only for a couple of hours a month. Over time, those couple of hours can add up. There are so many ways you can volunteer your time; just use your imagination and try to do something that is unique from the next person so you can stand out in a positive way.

Certificates / Licenses:

Don't list all 100 of the certificates you've received. Pick about five of your most important selling points (EMT, Firefighter 1 Academy, Firefighter 1, Paramedic, CPR, Class "B" Firefighter's Drivers License, Rescue Systems 1, etc.). The reason I put the word "license" in there is because Paramedic is a license, as well as a driver's license. The rest are certificates. Don't list your Class "C" (Standard Motor Vehicle license in California) Driver's license on the resume. It is a waste of space—it is already on the application. Only list unique licenses that are above and beyond what the average person might possess. Which one do I list first? The one that you feel is most important, then working downwards in order of importance.

When listing each certificate or license, <u>at the most</u>, you only need three things:

1. Exact name/title (as taken from the certificate or license).
2. Who certified you (as taken from the certificate or license).
3. When it expires or when you took it (as taken from the certificate or license). Expiration dates are extremely important with medical related cards such as CPR or EMT. That initial date you took the EMT class four years ago makes it look like you're expired if you only list your initial date you completed the class.

NOTE: Depending on your available space, you may only have the room to put #1 above—the exact name/title from your certificate or license. If that's the case, so be it.

Special Skills / Training:

Do you speak, read, and/or write a second language fluently? If so, list it here. I don't know of a fire department that wouldn't want someone that was fluent in a second language. Some fire departments in Southern California actually require second language fluency, in addition to EMT and Firefighter 1 just to take the entry-level firefighter test (and they get plenty of candidates!).

I can't think of too many other things to put under this heading. Not everyone will probably use this heading, but if you do—it might be something that goes towards the top of your resume. Stay away from things such as "I get along well with others." Last time I checked, a human being was expected to get along well with others. It is a "fluffy" statement that really has no relevance since it can't be backed up and sounds generic.

SUMMARY:

Which of the above "major headings" should you list first? Obviously the Objective should always be listed first. As for what goes next, I would suggest the one that is your strongest point, and then work downwards in importance. Why? Because the average person reads from the top down; so if you list it up towards the top, the perception is that it should be important. The farther something is towards the bottom of the page, the more it might be overlooked or seem unimportant. About the only thing I wouldn't list first would be my education. I had a four-year degree when I started testing, but I quickly realized that I needed to bury it in the middle of the page or the bottom. It is not that I was ashamed of it, it was that I didn't want to come across as a "college kid that was better than everyone on the panel and wanted to go straight to fire chief."

Having a four-year degree (or higher) is very commendable and valuable for the fire service as the level of education required for promotion continues to increase; just be careful you don't "oversell it." Mention and acknowledge that you have it, and that you want to be the best probationary firefighter that you can be; just don't dwell on it. It is possible that the people on the oral panel do not have that level of education; so don't come across like you are better than them. You are not—they have the job and you don't.

# # # #

Sample Resume #1:

Thomas C. Smith
1234 First Avenue – Chabot, CA, 99999 – (515) 867-5309

OBJECTIVE:	To serve as a Firefighter/Paramedic with the Oakland Fire Department

EXPERIENCE:

02/10 – Present
EMT - Paramedic
American Medical Response West, San Leandro, CA
Respond safely to EMS calls, perform patient transfers and assessments within county protocol and industry standards; maintain and expand my EMS knowledge and skills; provide exceptional customer service.

01/13 – Present
Firefighter Work Experience Student - Alameda County F.D.
Chabot College, Hayward, CA
Maximize available time and resources available to improve upon my base knowledge and skills in modern fire service operations. Learn role and responsibilities of a firefighter. Over 1,000 volunteer hours of service.

01/09 – Present
Instructional Assistant II (EMT)
Chabot College, Hayward, CA
Utilizing multimedia presentations, instruct and test students on the required skills, knowledge, and abilities to become outstanding EMTs; provide students with a positive role model.

05/08 – 02/09
Emergency Medical Technician
American Medical Response West, San Leandro, CA

11/02 – 12/06
Rifleman/Food Service Specialist, Corporal, USMC
Navy and Marine Corps Reserve Center, Alameda, CA

EDUCATION:

10/09 – Present
Bachelor of Science – Fire Technology (expected completion 12/14)
Cogswell Polytechnical College, Sunnyvale, CA

08/07 – 08/09
Associate of Arts Degree - Fire Technology
Chabot College, Hayward, CA

CERTIFICATES / LICENSES:
- EMT & Paramedic
- Firefighter 1 State Certification
- Firefighter 1 Academy
- ACLS / PALS / PHTLS / CPR / CPR Instructor
- I-100 / I-200 / I-300 / IS-700 / IS-800b
- Rescue Systems 1
- Haz Mat First Responder Operational
- S-212 / S-234 / S-270 / S-290 / S-390

COMMUNITY SERVICE:
- Over 100 hours of volunteer service with the American Red Cross, Hayward, CA
- Over 250 hours of volunteer service with the Boy Scouts of America, Fremont, CA

Sample Resume #2:

LAWRENCE S. JOHNSON	(555) 555-1234 - Home
1234 Martin Luther King Jr. Way	(555) 555-4321 - Mobile
Anycity, CA 99999	ljohnson@yahoo.com

OBJECTIVE:

- *To become a Firefighter for the City of Acme Fire Department*

EXPERIENCE:

Alameda County Fire Department, San Leandro, CA   *January 2013 to Present*
- **Student Firefighter**

   Significant Accomplishments:
   - Over 1200 hours of volunteer service completed through the Chabot College Fire Technology Work Experience program.

Safeway Stores, Inc., Oakland, CA
- **Senior Department Manager**   *April 2009 to Present*
- **Department Manager**   *May 2007 to April 2009*
- **Clerk/Cashier**   *September 2003 to May 2007*

   Significant Accomplishments:
   - Over 10 years of customer service experience without a day missed due to illness or injury.

EDUCATION:

Chabot College, Hayward, CA   *January 2013*
- **Associate of Arts Degree (A.A.)** in Fire Service Technology

CERTIFICATES:

- **Fire Fighter I Academy**, Chabot College
- **EMT**, Alameda County EMS Agency *(expires December 2014)*
- **CPR Healthcare Provider,** American Heart Association *(expires December 2014)*
- **Public Education 1**, California State Fire Marshal's Office

VOLUNTEER EXPERIENCE:

Boy Scouts of America, San Leandro, CA   *January 2011 to Present*
- **Volunteer Program Coordinator**

   Significant Accomplishments:
   - Over 3300 hours of volunteer service in a variety of areas including mentoring youth, providing training and education, and coordinating volunteer activities and volunteer personnel.

CHAPTER 5

The Written Examination

The written examination is usually one of the first steps in the hiring process for a firefighter. Most fire departments require you to have at least a score of 70% to pass and continue in the hiring process. While most fire departments do not use your score on the written examination as a portion of your overall ranking on the hiring list, they do use it as a way of "weeding out" candidates and making the overall number of candidates in the hiring process more manageable. Regardless, you should still strive to get a score of at least 90% on every written examination, and further strive for scores in the 95% to 100% range.

While scoring well on the written examination does not necessarily mean you will be an excellent firefighter, it does mean that you will be able to continue in the hiring process to the next phase (usually the oral interview), and it does assist your score if the fire department does make the score of your written examination a portion of your overall score (some fire departments have been known to make the written examination 50% of your total score and the oral interview the other 50% of your score, which is why you should be striving for the high 90 percentile). Also, even if 70% is the minimum passing score, some departments only take the highest written examination scores to continue in the hiring process (sometimes 85% to 90% or higher).

Most departments start out by giving the candidate a multiple choice examination, typically consisting of 100 questions focusing on math, English, understanding oral or written communications, mechanical ability, following directions, map reading, and interpersonal ability. If a department requires you to have more than entry-level qualifications (such as EMT, paramedic, Firefighter 1, etc.), there is a good chance you may see questions relating to those qualifications on the written examination. If they do not require those certifications, then they will most likely not test you on those subjects (if they want to stay out of court). Most departments use 70% as the passing point for the written examination. Not passing the written examination means that you don't go any farther and are not going to be considered for the duration of this hiring list (which can be a few years). You are definitely welcome to test with them in the future when a new hiring list is being created, but until then, you are out of luck.

However, don't think that a 70% score is sufficient. Many departments can do one of two things:

1. Use the written examination score as part of your overall ranking (i.e., 50% of your final score is from your written examination, 50% of your score is from your oral interview). Not having a written examination score of at least 95% will almost doom your chances of getting hired, even with a good oral interview score. Yes, it is that competitive.

2. Only accept a written examination score over a certain percentage to continue in the process. For example, 2,000 people may have passed with at least 70%, but the department only wants to send 500 people to the next phase. If the 500th best score on the written was an 88%, then they will only take folks with an 88% score or higher on the written examination. So, you may have passed with an 87% score, but it is not good enough to continue.

What is the moral of the story? Shoot for the high 90 percentiles on your written examinations if you want to be successful.

Before we go any further, I should mention that some departments are actually now using a different form of a written examination—that of a video-based assessment that evaluates the same type of subject areas that a typical written examination evaluates: reading comprehension, math, mechanical ability and even human behavior among other things.

National Testing Network (NTN) is a testing service that offers the candidate a major benefit:

- The ability to take one test and be eligible for hundreds of openings at numerous departments across the country (when this was written, there happened to be 170 different fire departments using this service. Meaning if you wanted to work for any of those departments, you could only do so by applying through NTN).

NTN is an alternative to the traditional written test that most fire departments have used and seems to be more popular every day. Instead of the candidate taking an actual written examination with pencil and paper, they offer a video-based test (known as the FireTEAM test) that I have evaluated and believe has a lot of value for a fire department to use as a screening tool for candidates.

My department recently tried it and overall I am pleased with the results. I did talk to a number of candidates who failed it and were obviously not happy with the process, as opposed to what they had been used to in the past with the traditional written examination. But, change can be tough—especially if you're not fully prepared for what to expect. If you go to their website, they do offer a practice test that would be worth your investment to at least get an idea of what to expect when you do take it for the first time. When I asked my students at the college what they thought of the video based test, those that passed obviously felt it was a very appropriate and applicable test. Not surprisingly, those that failed found fault in the process—as they would have probably found fault with had it been an actual written examination or anything else for that matter.

There are currently four components NTN uses to evaluate candidates, all of which are done via video at a computer workstation at a central location:

1. A video-based human relations test;
2. A mechanical aptitude test;
3. A math test;
4. A reading ability test

All four of those components are usually found on the typical fire service entry-level written examination. At the end of the day, the process seems fair, reasonable and appropriate to evaluate entry-level firefighter candidates and to use as a screening tool to determine who goes to the next phase of the hiring process, which is typically the oral interview.

# # # #

Frequently Asked Questions (FAQ)
About The Written Exam

What is the weight of the written exam in your overall ranking on the hiring eligibility list?

Either pass or fail with 70 % being the normal passing score, or a percentage of your overall score as compared to another component of the hiring process such as the oral interview. For example, a department may require all candidates to pass the written exam with at least a 70% score. That written exam score will make up 50% of your final score, with the oral interview score making up the other 50% of your final score—with the written and the oral scores being averaged together. But, don't just shoot for a 70 or 80 percent score. Why? Because some departments choose to only take the top written scores to the next phase of the hiring process and I've seen those top scores being 90 or 95% and above!

What are the main purposes of utilizing written tests?

Many people (including myself) will agree that written tests are not the best way to measure someone's knowledge of a certain subject or their ability as to whether they will be a perfect fit for the position and/or the department. However, written tests are commonly used for the following reasons:

1. As a weeding-out mechanism. It is not uncommon to see hundreds, if not thousands, of people applying for a couple of firefighter openings. By putting a minimum passing score of say, 70% on a written examination, it will weed out many of the candidates who are not ready or are unprepared. It is very expensive to put on a firefighter testing process, because of all of the staff time before, during, and after the process.

2. They are easy to grade. Utilizing a written test that is usually multiple-choice, is very easy to grade. Using a scantron form,

they can easily be put through a machine that grades them and also provides useful data for the people that are administering it, such as average score, overall scores for each individual question, etc.

3. They are easy to administer. To hold a written test, all that is usually required is one large auditorium, and a few folks to register people, and to walk around to ensure no cheating is occurring. Depending on the size of the auditorium and the number of candidates, it is sometimes possible to only have one time to have to administer the written test (versus a physical ability test or an oral interview, both of which require multiple times and dates since only one candidate is getting evaluated at a time.

Who puts together the written test?

In my experience, most fire departments do not put together their own written test. It is typically not cost effective to do so, based on the time and effort it takes to create a valid and reliable test, two important features when creating a test. There are many different private companies out there that produce entry-level firefighter written tests in use today. Three examples of such companies include:

- Cooperative Personnel Services (CPS)—http://www.cps.ca.gov
- Donnoe & Associates—http://www.donnoe.com
- National Testing Network—http://nationaltestingnetwork.com

What subject areas are the written tests typically testing you for?

The most common subjects (also known as dimensions) that an entry-level firefighter written test will cover include:

- Understanding oral directions
- Reading comprehension and understanding written information
- Understanding written instructions

- Numerical skills
- Mechanical aptitude/reasoning
- Memory and understanding oral information
- Teamwork
- Math ability
- Map or diagram reading
- Customer service
- Public Relations
- Community living

Some fire departments may also add supplemental questions in addition to the subject matter areas above. For example, the company CPS mentioned above offers fire departments supplemental tests that are in addition to the subjects listed above, to measure different areas that are specific to the position you are applying for. Some of these additional subjects can include:

- EMT
- Paramedic
- Report writing
- Incident Command System (ICS)
- National Incident Management System (NIMS)
- Ground ladder practices
- Fire Investigator
- Plan Review
- Aerial apparatus
- Firefighter essentials
- Fire inspection and code enforcement
- Uniform Fire Code

NOTE: If a fire department does not require a candidate to possess certain qualifications such as EMT or ICS as mentioned above, then they should not be testing you for such knowledge because it would be inappropriate to do so.

How long do I usually get to take an entry-level firefighter written test?

Most departments typically allow a candidate anywhere from two to three hours to complete the written test. That is why it is extremely important to pace yourself, and not take too much time. It is not uncommon to see many candidates with unanswered questions when they call "time is up" and direct you to turn in your test and answer sheet (regardless of whether or not you have completed it).

How many questions are typically on an entry-level firefighter test?

100

What types of questions are typically on entry-level firefighter tests?

Multiple choice are the most common questions you will find. The two main reasons why departments use this format are because they are easy to grade and there is less of a chance of guessing (if the question is written properly) because you have more choices to pick from.

True-false tests are typically not utilized because of the guessing factor (you have a 50% chance of picking the correct answer, even if you do not know anything about the subject matter, and because it is really hard to write a really discriminatory true-false question).

Essay tests are typically not used because of the time it takes to grade them as well as the subjectivity of their nature.

What is the anatomy of a multiple-choice test?

Typically, there are four or five choices to pick from in a multiple-choice test. First, there is the "stem" of the question. The stem is the first part of the question that is asking you something. There is usually one answer that is MOST correct, and then there are three or four other answers that are incorrect. Those incorrect answers are known as "distracters." If properly written, they are intended to distract you into thinking they are the correct answer.

It is very common to hear people after they have completed a test say "I didn't like the test, there were too many answers that were similar and very close." Well, from a test-maker's point of view, that is probably a good test. Why? Because there were no clear-cut answers.

If you can immediately pick out an answer to a multiple choice test, it should be because you have properly prepared yourself, not because of an easy, give-away answer.

I thought discrimination was illegal; why is it that a test is meant to discriminate?

Well, a good test discriminates between those that have prepared and those that have not prepared. Not all forms of discrimination are bad, as you can now see.

What are some different tips to do my best when taking a written test?

PRIOR TO THE TEST:

1. Make sure you are well rested. It is well known that fatigue does not help you stay alert or remain focused. If you have a job that requires you to work the night before (less than 12 hours before) a written test, try to get out of working (legitimately of course, definitely don't call in sick—that does not show good ethics or integrity). Don't be out late the night before a written test with your friends or indulge in alcohol.
2. Make sure you have eaten a light meal prior to the test. Plan to be in the auditorium taking your test for up to 3 hours. The last thing you want to distract you is a growling stomach, a full bladder, or a urgent bowel movement.
3. Make sure you know where you are going before the start of the test. Carefully read the notice that was sent to you that directs

you to the written test location. What you assume may not be exactly what is stated on the piece of paper. If you have never been there before, take the time to do a "dry-run" in advance to know how long it takes you to get there. Don't forget to factor in possible traffic, roadwork, accidents, poor weather, etc.; all of which can cause you to be late. It's always better to be early than late.

4. Make sure you properly prepare yourself to do your best on the test. If the department provides a study guide, MAKE SURE YOU MEMORIZE IT! If the department does not provide a study guide free-of-charge, but does offer one for purchase at a nominal price, spend the money to get it. You will probably find it to be worth the cost!

5. Make sure you bring ALL of the required items you are asked to bring. Most of the time, a department will provide all of the required test materials for the candidates (pencils, scantron forms, the notification letter, etc.). However, don't be the one idiot that forgets to bring required items (such as your driver's license, or a number two pencil). Having to go home and get your driver's license will probably not be an option since there will probably not be adequate time to do so. There is also no guarantee they will let you do so. Additionally, having to ask others for a pencil can be pretty embarrassing.

6. Talk with other candidates in line with you to be friendly. However, don't get intimidated by what you hear them say. It is not uncommon to overhear candidates telling other candidates how much experience or education they have, who they know, who their dad is, etc. Some of the things they say can make you feel like you don't stand a chance in hell to get hired, and are unqualified. It didn't take me long when I was testing to figure out that these loudmouths were really not my competition. They might have been able to talk the talk, but when it came time to walking the walk, they couldn't do it.

ONCE YOU ARE AT THE TEST LOCATION:

1. Be polite and courteous to EVERYONE you come in contact with. It is really a small world. I remember taking a written test and seeing a very large individual walking in a suit next to all of us that were sitting in line waiting to be let in. One of my acquaintances made a comment something to the effect of "who is that and how did he find someone to make a suit that big?" I swear it seemed like that person immediately looked in the direction of the person who made the comment, but didn't do anything else. It was one of those "if looks could kill" situations. By the way, that person actually turned out to be the department's fire chief! Who would have thought? How would you like to be the person sitting in a fire chief's interview face-to-face with the chief a few months later? What are the odds the chief would even remember who they were? Probably slim. However, if it was me who made a comment, I would be pretty nervous, even if I was pretty sure he didn't remember who I was. It just isn't worth risking.

2. Listen attentively to ALL of the direction you are provided. It never ceased to amaze me the number of candidates that were talking with each other while directions were being provided. You might miss something important like "don't leave your seat without raising your hand," "if you go to the bathroom, turn in your test materials to a proctor," "you have so much time to take the test," etc. Remember that you are getting evaluated on following directions. Failure to do so can lead to your disqualification.

3. Keep the talking to a minimum. If the test has not yet begun, you may miss important directions. If the test has begun, even if you are not cheating, it can and probably will appear that you are, which could lead to your being disqualified from the process.

4. Do not open up the test booklet until you are told to. Once again, you are getting evaluated on following directions; doing

this can lead to a proctor taking your test booklet and requesting you to leave the test site. Thank you for playing, Johnny tell him what he could have won.

5. Make sure you read all of the instructions in the beginning, throughout, and at the end of the test booklet. They are there for a purpose and a reason. Nothing worse than asking a question of a proctor and hearing them say "didn't you read the test booklet?"

6. Read each test question carefully. Missing one word can mean the difference between the right answer and the wrong answer. I've caught myself doing this and getting wrong answers on various occasions. I start reading the stem of the question and go straight to the answer I think is the right one, without having completely read the question. Bad move, proven over and over.

7. Before you answer the question, make sure you read ALL of the possible choices. Immediately picking the first one you see that looks right can be devastating.

8. Be wary of words in the question or answer that are absolute, such as shall, must, always, will, never, only, nobody, nothing, none, etc. Those are typically wrong because very little is absolute in life, except for death and taxes.

9. Make the effort to watch your time. Typically the proctors will announce when there is certain time frames remaining, such as one hour, 45 minutes, 30 minutes, 15 minutes, 2 minutes, etc. Be proactive and take responsibility for yourself. Take a look at your watch or the clock on the wall to keep track of your time. Remember the time they said, "go" and remember the time they stated will be the time they will say "stop." These items are usually announced in the beginning, just before you are allowed to start, while they are reading the instructions. If you are halfway through the allotted time, and you have more than half of the questions remaining to be answered, get a move on!

10. When you are not sure of the answer, there is a good way to make an educated guess. First, remember that it is very difficult to write a quality test (from a test-maker's point of view). Even

if you don't fully know the subject matter you are being tested on, it is possible much of the time to be able to narrow down your possible answers on a multiple choice test from four to two because of wording of the answers.

11. If you don't know an answer to a question, make a note of it on the scratch paper (assuming they provide you with one) and then come back to it later. Sometimes, if you don't know an answer at this moment, it may come to you after you have completed more questions, since some of the questions in a test are similar or give away an answer to another question.

12. Make sure you answer all of the questions. The majority of firefighter entry-level written tests do not penalize you for wrong answers. You typically only get penalized for wrong answers. What that means, is that you got nothing to lose by making a guess to a question that you don't know the answer to. With a multiple-choice question, you usually have a 25% of guessing the right answer (assuming there are four choices to pick from). To me, there is nothing worse than leaving an answer to a question blank. Take a chance and pick one of the choices.

13. Completely bubble in the correct answer on the answer form. In my years as an educator, I have noticed many answers to have been marked wrong either because the answer was not completely bubbled in or because the pencil marks ran over into another choice.

14. Don't mark in the test booklet, unless they tell you it is ok to do so. Also, don't make any extra marks on your test answer sheet because they may get mistaken for answer choices by the machine grading your test, and you'll never know about it.

15. Make sure you answer the questions in the correct order. We have all probably done this at one point or another. You go to answer question number 51 and by the time you hit question 71, you finally realize you have answered them out of order. Many times you get an answer sheet with more answer opportunities than there are questions. I remember one candidate when I was testing who must have realized his mistake after he answered

the last question and found out there were still some answer boxes left. He was scrambling so hard to erase the answers and put them in the right place that I don't think he was able to successfully do so by the time they said, "time is up."

16. If you do have to erase an answer, make sure you completely erase the answer you originally provided. Not doing so will potentially cause the machine grading your test to mistake the other answer as your first choice, causing you to get a wrong answer.

17. Always try to stick with the first answer that comes to your mind. Don't change your answer unless you are very sure that you are correct. Let me repeat that—very sure you are correct! I see it time and time again when reviewing graded test sheets—students missing the question that they had changed an answer to. Go with your gut instinct unless something clearly proves that instinct wrong.

WHEN YOU ARE DONE WITH YOUR TEST:

1. When you think you have finished, the first thing you should do is check your answer sheet for the following items:
   a. Make sure your name and other vital information is on there as requested.
   b. Make sure you have answered all of the questions, and that you don't have more than one answer for each question.
   c. Make sure there are no extra pencil marks on your scantron or in the test booklet.

2. Make sure you have listened to the directions provided or read the directions provided as to what to do when you have completed the test. Typically, you will be asked to bring all of your testing materials (test booklet, pencil, scantron, scratch paper, etc.) to a certain desk and to an actual person to evaluate. That person will make sure you do not leave the room with any testing materials.

3. When leaving the test room, I don't care how bad you think you may have screwed up. Do not, I repeat do not, start talking out loud about how bad you screwed up. Save it for when you get inside your car or until you are back home. It doesn't leave a positive impression about you. I've seen it happen.

4. When you get back to your car, have a scratch pad handy to write down as many of the test questions and answers that you can remember. Unless you are told by the proctors to not do this, or were told in the written instructions not to do this, then this is one way to improve your scores the next time you see the same test. If you are testing long enough, you will start seeing the same (or very similar) written tests. There are only so many different companies and versions out there. Build up a database for yourself to study from for the next time. Additionally, this is a great way to test your retention skills and to learn from your mistakes. When there were answers I didn't know what they were looking for on, I would ask different people whose opinions I trusted, how they would answer the question (after I gave them the answer I put down). I would then ask them how they got to that answer.

5. Wait patiently for your results. It is not uncommon to have to wait a couple of weeks (if not months) to get your results back. Do not bug them for the results. There are usually only a few people working in the personnel department, and remember that they are probably also doing other recruitments simultaneously. Don't call them and expect your results, they just don't have the time and effort to that for you. Results will not be given over the phone because of the time and effort it takes to do so and because of confidentiality reasons, there is really no way to be 100% sure you are who you say you are. Don't take it personally.

6. Now if you find out from some of your friends that they have received your results and you have not, then it is very possible your results may have been misplaced. Wait a couple of days (mail can be slow) and contact them at that point. Don't get mad or angry with the personnel folks; it will not help your situation,

regardless of how frustrated you may be. Remember—you may win the battle, but did you really win the war in the end? I will go out on a limb and say no!

BOOKS TO HELP YOU PREPARE:

There are numerous different books to assist you with preparing for a fire service written examination. Some sources to obtain firefighter preparation books include:

- The Firefighters Bookstore—http://www.firebooks.com
- FSP Books & Video—http://www.fire-police-ems.com
- Amazon—http://www.amazon.com

# # # #

CHAPTER 6

The Oral Interview

The oral interview is the most important phase of virtually every hiring process. Whether you are testing to become a firefighter or attempting to land a job in the business world, you still must realize that the oral interview is the phase of the hiring process that will determine whether you will get hired or not get hired. Many people argue that it isn't fair to base a hiring decision on a 15 or 30 minute oral interview. While I agree with them, I do realize that this is reality land and that many organizations base a majority of their hiring decision on that oral interview. That is why it is critical to do your best on the oral interview and also know what you are getting into when you walk into your interview; all so that you can achieve the most possible points.

Here are some answers to some of the questions I am most frequently asked regarding oral interviews:

Question: How many board members are usually on the oral interview panel?

Answer: You should expect anywhere from two members up to seven members on your oral panel; however the most common number appears to be three to five.

Question: Where do the board members usually come from?

Answer: Oral board members for the entry-level oral interview can either be from the fire department that is interviewing or neighboring fire departments. Most entry-level oral interview boards are typically made up of individuals from the rank of firefighter up through the rank of battalion chief. There is also usually a member of the city or department's personnel or human resourced department in the interview, to moderate it and ensure everyone is on their best behavior and not asking inappropriate questions. Some fire departments do have members from neighboring fire departments assist them as evaluators, to help ensure impartiality and objectivity. Some fire departments even use citizens from the community to rate the candidates, so make sure that you answer your questions in a way that everyone can understand. Don't start spitting out all these fire service related acronyms that a citizen from the community or a personnel services manager might not have a clue about. If they don't know what you are talking about, you risk the chance of not getting the maximum points!

Question: When answering an oral board question, do I only make eye contact with the person who asked the question?

Answer: When answering questions, make sure that you make eye contact with <u>all</u> of the panel members, make sure that you include all of them in your presentation. Only looking at one of the panel members can alienate the others and is not professional.

Question: What types of questions could I expect on the entry-level oral interview?

Answer: When I was testing for the position of firefighter, many departments were still asking questions specific to EMT and Firefighter 1 curriculum. Very few departments ask those specific questions anymore. However, be prepared—if the department is requiring a certain license or certificate to take the test, it is still highly possible that they will ask you those types of questions on the oral interview.

If they really wanted to stump people and find out who really knows their stuff (as opposed to many candidates who just get the certificate or complete the class and then forget what they learned a month after it is over), they would ask questions such as "what are the signs and symptoms of hypothermia or heat exhaustion?" That would eliminate a lot of candidates, or at least separate the ones who have studied and retained the information versus the ones who have not.

However, most departments have a specific (a.k.a. standardized) set of basic questions they will ask you. Typical questions can include, but are not limited to:

- Why do want to become a firefighter for our department?
- What have you done to prepare yourself for the position of firefighter (also known as the opening statement)
- Tell us about yourself (also known as the opening statement).
- What do you know about our fire department?
- Why do you want to work for our fire department?
- What do you know about our city/county?
- What type of volunteer work do you currently perform?'
- What are your career goals?
- What is your five-year plan? Your ten-year plan?
- Why should we hire you over all the other candidates?
- What is your definition of cultural diversity?
- What is your definition of customer service?
- Give us an example of outstanding customer service you have provided.
- Name one word that best describes you.
- What does a firefighter do? Can you describe the daily routine?
- How would you handle yourself if faced with an angry customer on scene of a response?
- What are the three biggest issues facing the fire service today?
- Provide three critical functions a firefighter provides to the community.
- What are your strengths?

- What are your weaknesses; and what are you doing to improve those weaknesses?
- Questions asking you to describe a situation from your past where you have made a situation better (relating to a work project or accomplishment or a personnel issue).
- Questions to test your tolerance, ethics, or values relating to stealing, alcohol, drugs, cheating, unethical behavior, harassment, conflicting orders, ability to play nicely with others, etc.
- Questions to how you would handle yourself on the emergency scene.
- Questions to how you would handle yourself at the fire station.
- Is there anything else you have left out or would like to add (also known as the closing statement)

Question: Should I bring copies of all of my certifications / transcripts / accomplishments to the oral interview?

Answer: NO! If they want them, they will ask you for them. You will get your opportunity to provide them copies of everything when you go in for your background investigation. At the time of application, you should have provided ONLY the certificates that they requested you to provide. Think about what the oral panel has to do. They are there to grade you based on your responses to the questions. They are attempting to listen and watch you. They do not have the time to sort through mounds of paperwork. Paperwork proves you completed the class, it doesn't prove that you can communicate well enough to score the highest on each question.

Question: Should I bring a resume to the oral interview?

Answer: You should have included a resume to your application at the time of filing. The only reason you should attempt to provide the oral panel with a resume if you didn't have the opportunity to do at the time of application or if there have been MAJOR updates or changes to it. Otherwise, the oral board has enough paperwork in front of them anyway to juggle. Ideally, if you have made a lot of changes because of more certificates, different jobs, etc. try to get it to the fire department or personnel / human resources department in advance so they can make copies for all of the oral board members. That way they can have it to look at prior to you walking in the room (which leaves them virtually no time to look at it).

Question: How long should I expect the oral interview to last?

Answer: It is my experience that most oral interviews typically last anywhere from 15 minutes to 30 minutes. I have had and heard of entry-level oral interviews that have lasted as little as 8 minutes and as long as 45 minutes.

Question: What percentage of my overall score on the final hiring/ eligibility list is based on my oral interview score?

Answer: Most departments today make your oral interview 100% of your overall score / ranking on the hiring / eligibility list. A few departments still put your written examination score as 50% of your final score and your oral interview as the other 50% of your final score. 100% of your score depends on those 15 to 30 minutes of you selling yourself in front of a board of possible strangers. This is why the oral interview is the most important phase to prepare yourself for!

Question: What behaviors, traits, and/or characteristics (more commonly known as dimensions) will the oral board be rating me on?

Answer: The most common "dimensions" are as follows:

- Oral communications
- Problem solving ability
- Decision making ability
- Maturity
- Leadership
- Preparation for the position

- Interpersonal ability
- Technical competence
- Knowledge of the position

Question: How should I best prepare for the oral interview?

Answer: Proper preparation includes doing your homework and research well in advance of your interview, not starting the day before. You should have even started to begin your fire department information library well before that fire department even opened up their testing process. Every fire department is going to hire again sometime in the future. When you come across information that might be relevant should you ever test with that department, file it away for the future!

The best five ways to prepare for the oral interview are as follows:

1. Stop by fire stations to talk with the firefighters that are already employed there.
2. Stop by city hall (or the county building if is a county fire department) to obtain information about the city or county demographics.
3. Go to the fire department website and see what valuable information you might find (might be different than what you obtained in person).
4. Go to the city or county website to see what information you can find about the city or county that the fire department is located in (might be different than what you obtained in person).
5. Drive around the area that the fire department protects so that you can see for yourself what type of area you are applying for.

All of those above items are great things to talk about if you are ever asked the question "what have you done to prepare yourself" or "what do you know about the city or fire department?"

# # # #

8 Tips To Successfully Prepare For
Your Upcoming Oral Interview

The question is not if you will have an upcoming oral interview, but when your interview will be. This is something most candidates don't get and don't take seriously enough. Too many candidates wait until the last minute to prepare for their oral interview, which usually works to their disadvantage.

In most fire departments, the oral interview score usually accounts for 100% of your overall score and ranking on the hiring list. Therefore, it is extremely important and critical that you properly prepare yourself for the oral interview. Many people can just "wing-it" on a written examination or physical ability test. However, it can be very difficult to "wing-it" during your oral interview, especially if you have not completely prepared yourself. If you have not completely put the time and effort into the process, than you are only wasting their time and yours. Based on my experiences and observations, here are some tips to help you successfully prepare for the oral interview:

Tip #1: Know where you are going before you get there.

I realize this is easier said than done. I think of myself as pretty good with directions, which means I don't necessarily always look at maps; most of the time that works out for the better. Regardless, not looking at maps came back to bite me a few times while I was testing. One time, I was driving about one hour to take an oral interview that I had assumed would be located at the community center (because it was held there last year when I had also taken their oral interview). Guess what, I was wrong! I get to the community center and it was all locked up.

I ended up driving by a fire station (which was coincidentally located by the community center, otherwise I would have been in trouble since I had not brought a map with me) and the crew did not know where the oral interview was going to be occurring (I realize that seems odd, but many departments do not inform their members of information relating to the testing process). I was basically out of luck since the time for the test had already come and gone. What is the moral of the story? I should have taken the letter the city had sent me with the location of the testing site with me that day. I should have also looked at that letter more closely well in advance. I would have still had plenty of time to get an actual printed map from AAA or a convenience store or even download directions from one of the online mapping providers (old school method – great back-up when the electronic device doesn't work or navigates you to the wrong place), or rely on your smart phone or GPS device and take your chances – don't do the same mistake as I did!

Tip #2: Have your attire already prepared and ready to use on the day of the interview.

There is nothing worse than getting dressed for an interview and finding out that your dress shirt is still at the cleaners, or actually needs to go to the cleaners because it is wrinkled or dirty. The same goes with the rest of your dress attire. As soon as you get the notice in the mail for the interview, get your clothes ready. I also suggest having more than one dress shirt and tie so that if you damage one or get one dirty, you always have at least one backup. Also, if you are really putting some time and effort into testing, you are going to find yourself at times having more than one interview in a week (sometimes in a day)! Don't wear the same dirty shirt to the next interview; take it to the cleaners and wear your backup shirt!

Tip #3: Leave plenty of time to get to the location of the interview.

This ties into tip number one above, know where you are going before you get there. When I was testing, I was not the best at leaving plenty of time to get somewhere (for that matter, I really am that way in a lot of things in life; I do make it to work on time though). Because of my last minute leaving, I was late for a couple of written tests, and they did not let me in. For one of those, I drove an hour and a half for nothing. Could I have prevented that? Of course I could have. If possible, drive to the testing site in advance, to see how long it will take you. Once you have determined your estimated time of travel, double that time just to leave yourself some "flex-time" in case of car trouble, auto accidents, traffic delays, etc.

Tip #4: Do as much homework / research on the position as you can, well in advance of the interview.

If it is worth your time and effort to drive to the test and participate in the hiring process, than it is worth your time and effort to actually spend some time doing your homework on the agency you are testing for. One time I proctored a Volunteer / Reserve Firefighter oral interview for our Department. When they were asked questions relating to how they would be utilized as a Volunteer / Reserve Firefighter, the majority of candidates answered the questions without any knowledge of how we would be utilizing them.

Many of them answered that when their pager went off, that they would respond to the fire station and then go out to the call to go do some firefighting. Well, our Department does not operate that way. They would be expected to respond to the incident scene and would then be utilized more often than not in a support fashion, not in a primary offensive firefighting fashion. Had they done their homework by researching the fire department and how the rank they were applying for operated, they would have been able to answer the questions better and increase their chances of getting a better score on the interview.

How can you research the department? Almost every fire department has a website that has some information relating to the department on it. Every fire department has firefighters that are usually very willing to assist the candidate that is attempting to work for them. Those are probably the two most important ways to find out more about not just the agency you are applying to, but the position you are applying for as well.

Tip #5: Get plenty of sleep the night before the interview.

It has been proven time and time again that we all should strive for eight hours of sleep per night. Some of you are able to survive on less; some are able to survive on more. You know yourself better than anyone else does. Don't go out partying the night before an interview (or any phase of the testing process for that matter) and expect to perform at 100%. If nothing else, you are probably still going to be off gassing any of the alcohol you might have consumed (assuming you had your two beers) and it will probably be very noticeable to the department representatives. Showering, throwing on perfume or cologne (whatever your poison might be), and putting on clean clothes can only do so much improvement to you.

Tip #6: Practice answering questions with your audio-recorder/video-recorder.

This is something that many candidates don't take advantage of, and I don't know why. Recording devices are a relatively cheap investment into your future that you can use for the rest of your life, and in areas besides firefighting. Most of us probably think we are excellent at oral communications. You will continue thinking that until you hear yourself speaking. The first time I heard myself, I didn't think it sounded like me at all. Then I heard myself answer some questions and it really humbled me and pointed out some obvious communication issues I needed to improve. Video-recorders are even better because they bring out your body language and mannerisms that you present. You might be able to find out that you have many bad or nervous habits that you were not even aware of by watching yourself through a video-recorder.

Tip #7: Know yourself inside and out, and be able to talk about yourself inside and out.

The oral interview panel is grading you based on your answers to the questions. If you do not completely answer the question, you do not get the most possible number of points. The oral has no clue who you are or what you have done to prepare for the position. Be able to bring out all of your strengths and positive attributes, as well as your past accomplishments and contributions. Be able to talk about your weaknesses (yes, we all have them) and what you are doing to improve them. I hear many candidates say they are uncomfortable talking about themselves. Well, if that is your case, either get over it and find a way to be comfortable, or do not expect to ever score high enough to get hired. Remember, there is a fine line between being overconfident and being cocky or arrogant. Learn to find a happy medium. You're there to market and sell your most important product—you!

Tip #8: Key points to be successful when answering oral interview questions.

- Pause; don't immediately go into your answer. Take time to absorb the question before blurting out your response.
- Don't use words such as uh, uhm, ah, ok, you know, etc.
- Don't be monotone!
- Module your voice tone and pitch.
- Be enthusiastic!
- Don't use excessive hand movements.
- Watch your body language.
- Don't just answer the question; answer the question! Be detailed, not brief in your answer. You will almost never be asked a one-word answer since the oral board wants to hear your thoughts. If you state a fact, make sure you back it up with an example. For example, don't just say I'm loyal. Prove it. Instead, state something like "I am loyal because I have been with the same employer for the last ten years." Wow, that proves your point and convinces the oral board you walk the walk and talk the talk.
- Make eye contact with all oral board members.
- Do not ramble; instead, take them on a journey, but make sure you have a destination in mind!
- Manage your time.
- Try to have unique, personalized answers.

- Do not apologize for anything!

Tip #9: Key points to succeed at your next oral interview.

- Know what is on your application and resume.
- Know the requirements, as well as the duties and responsibilities of the position (found on the job announcement).
- Know the fire department.
- Know the community.
- Know what you have done.
- Know where you are going (both career wise and location wise).
- Know what you can and cannot do.
- Visualize answers to each question.
- Rehearse your answers—practice, practice, and practice!
- Use a video recorder and/or audio recorder to see and/or hear yourself.
- Know the culture of the fire department you're applying for (if you have not figured it out by now, each department has it's own unique culture—good, bad or indifferent).
- When you are done, make sure you write down the questions you were asked when you get back to your car you may see them again.
- Try to remember the names/ranks of the personnel on your oral board. You never know when you'll meet them again.
- Make sure you use key words and phrases that show you have an above average understanding of the fire service. But, be careful—make sure you know what the word or phrase means because you may be asked what the definition is!
- Have a story to tell, and a situation to draw from, for virtually every type of question you may be asked.
- Plan on arriving at least 30 minutes early. Scout out your travel route in advance (not the same day, but days prior); ensure you know where you are going and where you need to park.

- Do not arrive too early; you may just wear out your welcome and be an annoyance if you cannot keep your mouth shut or if you say the wrong things.
- Regarding attire, have at least two different sets of dress shirts, ties, socks, etc., in case you have two back-to-back interviews, and you don't have the chance to have them washed or cleaned.

Tip #10: Practice answering all of the potential oral interview questions so that you are prepared for anything.

Some people say that they don't want to practice answering questions because they will sound like they are memorized or rehearsed. Duh! Practicing will make you sound more organized, more complete and thorough (because you will minimize leaving important things out of your speech), and like a better communicator. There are not that many different types of oral interview questions that you can be asked. Most departments just want to find out who you are, what your background consists of, how your background will make you a perfect fit for that department, what your ethics or values are, why you want to work for that department, how well you will get along with others and how well you will follow orders and/ or directions.

Start doing some research on the internet and you can start finding out different types of questions. Also, when you finish an interview, take the time to write out the questions when you get back to the car (unless they tell you not to do so) so that you can practice that question for the future. Take the time to build a catalog of oral board questions and your potential answers to the questions. Then you can take them to people that have sat on oral boards before and get their opinions. Be careful though, everyone has an opinion— good, bad, or indifferent!

SUMMARY:

Taking the time now to prepare for any and all of your upcoming oral interviews should pay off in the long run. Most firefighters and individuals involved with the hiring process will probably agree that the oral interview is the most important phase of the hiring process. They are making a decision whether to hire you based on a 15 or 30-minute interview. Make the most of that time through proper preparation and you should see your scores drastically improve!

# # # #

Oral Interview Grading Sheets

There are different types of scoring sheets or scoring scales a fire department will utilize to evaluate a candidate's oral interview experience. Most departments utilize some form of grading scale to determine a candidate's performance during the oral interview, which will ultimately determine where on the hiring eligibility list a candidate will end up, especially since the oral interview typically makes up 100% of the overall ranking on the eligibility list. One such example is a rating scale like we are used to seeing in school, of A, B, C, D and/or F, where a C is barely passing, an A is perfect, and a D or an F is failing. Another example is a percentage scale of 0 to 100, with 70 percent as the minimum passing score.

How each department may ask their raters to rate candidates can also differ. In some departments, each question may have an individual score that will be added up, or the department may just ask the rater to assign an overall whole number as an overall average of all of the questions answered. The grading sheets will typically ask the rater to evaluate each candidate based on their answers to the questions, as compared to the individual dimensions, behaviors, and/or traits that are being evaluated during the oral interview. The most common dimensions are as follows:

- Oral communications
- Problem solving ability
- Decision making ability
- Maturity
- Leadership
- Preparation for the position
- Interpersonal ability
- Technical competence
- Knowledge of the position

Sample Oral Interview Grading Sheet #1:

Candidate Name: _____

Rater Name: _____

Date: _____

Dimension Evaluated	Score	Total
Oral communication	60 – 65 – 70 – 75 – 80 – 85 – 90 – 95 – 100	
Ability to use sound judgment and make critical decisions	60 – 65 – 70 – 75 – 80 – 85 – 90 – 95 – 100	
Background, preparation, motivation & knowledge of the fire service	60 – 65 – 70 – 75 – 80 – 85 – 90 – 95 – 100	
Ability to maintain cooperative work relationships	60 – 65 – 70 – 75 – 80 – 85 – 90 – 95 – 100	
• Total Score:	Note: *select a score that ends in a "5" or "0" only.*	
• Divide Total by 4		
FINAL SCORE		

Scoring Scale:

90 – 100   **Outstanding:** This candidate would be able to perform the duties and responsibilities of the position in an <u>outstanding</u> manner, and is <u>definitely</u> ready to go directly into the recruit academy and then the probationary period.

80 – 85   **Qualified:** This candidate would be able to perform the duties and responsibilities of the position in an <u>above average</u> manner, and is <u>probably</u> ready to go directly into the recruit academy and then the probationary period.

70 – 75   **Adequately Qualified:** This candidate would <u>probably</u> be able to perform the duties and responsibilities of the position in a <u>minimally acceptable</u> manner, and is <u>possibly</u> ready to go directly into the recruit academy and then the probationary period.

60 – 65   **Not Qualified:** This candidate is not yet ready for the position.

Comments:

_____
_____
_____
_____

Steve Prziborowski

Sample Oral Interview Grading Sheet #2:

Candidate Name: _____ **Rater Name:** _____

1. **INTERPERSONAL ABILITY:** The ability to work with others as part of a team and be reasonable in expressing opinions so as to avoid conflict with others. The willingness to accept commands without hesitation.

   Please check the appropriate box:

   Unacceptable   Acceptable   Above Average   Excellent
   ....

2. **MATURITY:** The willingness to make certain personal sacrifices while being of service to the community or meeting the objectives of the fire department. The ability to empathize with persons suffering from personal loss or injury. The ability to perform efficiently and effectively during an emergency. Capable of performing the same mental or physical activities without becoming bored or stressed. Awareness of the need for personal hygiene and clean living quarters in the fire station.

   Please check the appropriate box:

   Unacceptable   Acceptable   Above Average   Excellent
   ....

3. **JOB ORIENTATION:** The ability to maintain efficient performance under rapidly changing conditions and to develop alternative solutions to job-related problems by improvising when necessary. Has a desire to make the fire service a career and wants to advance in the fire service by taking courses and keeping job knowledge, skills, and abilities up-to-date.

   Please check the appropriate box:

   Unacceptable   Acceptable   Above Average   Excellent
   ....

4. **COMMUNICATION SKILLS:** The ability to relate to a variety of individuals and groups. The ability to deal with other department personnel, other city department employees, community residents and business people in order to influence them towards action or point of view. The ability to effectively orally communicate to ensure they can provide as well as receive and understand the intended message.

   Please check the appropriate box:

   Unacceptable   Acceptable   Above Average   Excellent
   ....

Overall Rating Scale:

90 - 100   Excellent: I feel this applicant would make an excellent employee and would be a definite asset to the fire department and to the community.

80 - 89   Above Average: I feel confident this applicant would make a good employee and be a positive asset to the fire department and to the community.

70 - 79   Average: I feel this applicant can satisfactorily perform the required duties of the position.

60 - 69   Unacceptable: I feel this applicant is unqualified for the position and I would not consider hiring them at this time.

_____   **Rater's overall score** (A number from 60 to 100, whole numbers only, no percentages)

Date: _____   Rater's Signature: _____

Remarks:

_____
_____
_____
_____

Oral Interviews: The Opening Statement

The opening statement of an oral interview is probably the most important opportunity you will be provided with to make a positive and lasting first impression. This is your chance to set the stage for the rest of your interview and to hit the ground running so that you can come out on the top of the final hiring list. Most fire departments grade the oral interview 100% of your total oral board score; starting out on the right foot with a solid opening statement can help you obtain a high score in the oral interview.

What is an opening statement? It is your chance to reduce the nervousness, to get a little comfortable (don't get too comfortable!), and to let the oral board know something about you—the most important person during the allotted time frame of your interview! An opening statement is your chance to provide the oral board with information about:

- Your personal characteristics, traits, beliefs, career goals, etc.
- Your educational background (formal education—don't include high school, it shows your age).
- Your training background (certifications, licenses, etc.)
- Your experience (paid and volunteer).
- Your special skills / talents (bilingual ability, mechanical ability background, etc.).
- Basically all of the information that you have listed on your resume (without being too specific that you bore them to death).

Your resume needs to be memorized and you need to be able to talk about all of the things you are offering to the department that makes you the best candidate for the job. Only you can properly market and sell yourself! Your opening statement is a way to get the oral board motivated to listen to what you have to say during the time you are being interviewed.

Examples of opening statement questions you will be asked include:

1. Tell us how you have prepared yourself for the position of

    _____.

2. Tell us how your education, experience, and training have prepared you for the position of _____.

3. Tell us about yourself.

I suggest you take the time to write out a response to each of the above questions (and the responses can be very similar and modified as needed) and then save them on your computer as a document you can modify as necessary. An opening statement is typically going to be anywhere between one and a half minutes up to about three minutes in length. Any less than that, and you're depriving the oral board of hearing as much as they can about your key attributes. Any more than that, and you risk the chance of boring them to death, putting them to sleep, or having them lose all interest in you and the rest of what you half to say.

A Chief Officer who is a friend of mine, stated he had recently sat on his Department's oral board panel for entry-level firefighters. I was asking him for some feedback regarding their interviews, so I could pass on some "lessons-learned of what not to do during an oral interview" to other folks. He stated they had one candidate with an opening statement lasting approximately 19 minutes. Then, a couple of days later, another candidate beat that record with one lasting almost 25 minutes! Even the person with the best resume in the world (I know, no such thing – the word best is subjective) can't fill 25 minutes worth of opening statement material. He told me he had lost interest at the point both candidates were about five minutes into their opening statements, but they had let the candidates continue anyway. They finally had to stop the second candidate because they were running out of time, and they still had more questions to ask, and more candidates to interview.

You want the oral board to remember you for being unique, in a positive way. These two candidates will be remembered for being unique, just not in a positive way. In case you were wondering, neither received job offers.

Since most oral interviews are on a tight schedule, it is paramount to use your time wisely! I had a time when I was interviewing for an entry-level firefighter position with the City of Daly City Fire Department and I was doing my typical three-minute opening statement. After about two minutes, one of the board members politely advised me that I had better be careful and cut my answer short because they still had four other questions to ask me, and that candidates were scheduled for every ten minutes! I reluctantly abbreviated my opening statement, summarizing the remaining information, and went on to answer the other questions. When I walked out, I thought I had blown the interview. Turns out, I ended up ranking number one on the hiring list (no ties that I was aware of); the only firefighter entry-level test I ever ranked number one on.

Having your opening statement on the computer is a valuable tool I am glad I utilized, and I will explain why. When I was testing for the position of firefighter over the course of 4 1/2 years, I probably had the opportunity to participate in approximately 50 oral interviews. While I didn't have an opening statement on the computer at the time, I did have it written down and virtually memorized. I had it down so well I could regurgitate it at a moment's notice, modifying it to fit the agency I was applying to.

Now before you say "I don't want to memorize an answer because it will sound rehearsed," wait a second. Having an answer memorized will make you sound like you have practiced and prepared for the interview. I would rather listen to someone that has practiced their opening statement than to someone who is just winging it or throwing things out at random and in no specific order. Lack of practice can increase your odds of leaving out key points about you.

I used to carry the opening statement with me to the oral interview and review it while waiting to be called. Realize there was no way I could memorize word-for-word the entire opening statement. That's ok; memorizing it allowed me to picture it in my head and ensure that I could cover the major points I wanted to cover, and ad-lib as needed to fill in the blanks. The nice part about having it on the computer is that I could change it as needed, cater it to the agency I was testing for, add accomplishments or achievements as I received them, delete things that were no longer applicable or appropriate, and alter it as necessary. Consider your opening statement as a work in progress.

When I was preparing for the Captain's promotional examination, I mistakenly did not spend as much time preparing for the oral interview as I initially thought I should. I think I became complacent and felt I could just "wing-it" and go with the flow when they asked me the question. I had spent countless hours preparing for the written examination, the personnel problem, the fire simulation, and for the position of Captain itself, but not that much time (if any) preparing my opening statement. Yes, I had prepared for other questions in the oral interview such as my strengths and weaknesses, programs the department was offering, various situations they could ask me, etc. However, I spent virtually no time preparing an opening (or closing) statement.

Luckily, I had an eye-opening experience that kicked me in the pants and forced me to go to my computer and create an opening (and closing) statement for the position of Captain. Something different from when I was testing for firefighter, primarily because I could not find the notes I had utilized at that point.

Here is that eye-opening experience that was embarrassing at the time it occurred, but very critical I believe to my overall success on the Captain's exam:

- About a month prior to the Captain's exam, our department had opened up a firefighter position in our training division, and I was very interested in applying for the position. I had been instructing classes for a while and I felt it would be a valuable position for career development purposes and also a position I could give something back to the department in (I had recently completed my Fire Instructor 1, 2 and 3 training through the State Fire Marshal's Office—240 hours of instructor training that now allowed me to not just instruct classes, but instruct the firefighters who aspired to be instructors within the department and the State Fire Marshal's instructional system).

- The process for the position of firefighter in training consisted of filing an application and completing an oral interview with the Training Captain and the EMS Coordinator. There was only one other person that had applied for the position, a firefighter with more experience and also prior training division experience (he had held the same spot about ten years prior). One day while working on shift at the fire house, the Training Captain called me up and asked if I wouldn't mind coming in that afternoon for an interview, since they wanted to complete the process before I went on vacation the next week. I said fine, and didn't think it would be that big of a deal, especially since he had told me that it would just be a casual / informal interview, and just a formality.

- I went into the interview thinking that it wouldn't be that big of a deal; I had done really well on oral interviews in the past, why should this one be any different? Famous last words! They started by asking me the standard opening statement question, "tell us how you have prepared for the position of firefighter assigned to the Training Division?" Here's my chance to shine, or so I thought. I was able to get about one sentence out of my mouth before I realized that I had not prepared, and I really did not have all of my qualifications packaged into a clean, well-prepared opening statement. I was so embarrassed at myself for not having an organized opening statement, that I had to stop my opening statement and apologize to both of the oral board members, both of whom I believed to have a great working relationship with and both of whom knew my qualifications well. Both of them told me to not worry about it, and to just continue on.

- Continue on I did. I answered the rest of the questions they asked me adequately, but not superbly. I ended up not getting the position, and I firmly believe it was because of my oral communication skills (or lack thereof) that I had presented that afternoon. Now I can live with not getting that position; what I could not live with was that in about two months, I was potentially going to have an oral interview for the position of Captain (assuming I made it that far in the assessment center).

- Had this been my Captain's oral interview, I would have been dead in the water. This was the epiphany that made me get my act together for the upcoming Captain's assessment center. Had I not had the opportunity to participate in that oral interview, I might have not seen my shortcomings and lack of preparation in time to secure a spot high enough on the Captain's promotional list to get promoted on my first try (which I did).

The one good thing that came out of that embarrassing moment above was that I went back to the firehouse that night and literally wrote out my opening statement and put it on computer!

It took me a couple of days to get it really where I wanted it to be—a positive and powerful representation of my key selling points. I was able to turn that embarrassing moment into a turning point in my preparation for the Captain's test. Because of that embarrassing moment, and the preparation that followed that moment, I ended up coming out number one (out of 11 candidates) in the assessment center, and also being the only candidate to score 100% in any phase of the assessment center. I scored 100% on my oral interview and I correlate that score primarily to the preparation I had done at the last minute, thanks to my "crashing and burning" at the other interview I had participated in for the training position. Had I not had that other interview, I strongly believe I might have fallen into the false sense of security that many candidates have with certain areas of their abilities.

**Below is the opening statement I used when
I took the Captain's examination:**

"Members of the board, I have been in the fire service for over 8 years, and with the Department for almost 5 years. I am presently assigned to Engine 11-serving the citizens of the City of Campbell as a Firefighter/Engineer-Paramedic. Let me take a few minutes and explain how my education, training and experience have prepared me for the position of Fire Captain.

First, regarding education, I have completed my B.S. degree with a major in Criminal Justice and a minor in Business Administration from California State University at Hayward, and also my A.A. degree in Fire Service Technology from Chabot College in Hayward. One thing that is not on my resume is that 2 weeks ago, I started working on a Master's Degree in Emergency Services Administration through California State University at Long Beach. It is being hosted by the San Jose Fire Department and should take 2 to 3 years to complete.

As for training, another addition that is not on my resume is that last month, I completed my last 2 chief officer classes through the California State Fire Marshal's office. Although I am competing for the position of Fire Captain, I believe completing the chief officer certification classes makes me more prepared for the position than just having done the fire officer certification classes (which I have already done). A mentor of mine, once told me to always prepare myself for one position above what I'm applying for, and this will allow me to be better prepared and better rounded.

Something else that is not on my resume is that in late May, I completed the Master Instructor course at the California State Fire Academy at Asilomar. There are only about 140 people in the state of California that are certified as Master Instructors. This certification allows me to teach Instructor 1A and 1B, the two required courses for firefighters that want to be certified by the California State Fire Marshal to teach within their respective fire departments or who want to become certified fire officers.

Certifications I have obtained through the California State Board of Fire Services include Fire Officer, Fire Instructor I and II, Public Education Officer, Fire Prevention Officer I, and Fire Investigator I. I have also completed various other California State Fire Marshal classes such as all three level two Fire Prevention classes and both level two Fire Investigation classes, just to provide me with a well-rounded background.

Now allow me to talk about experience. Some of the highlights of my almost five year career with this great Department include being a member of the Safety Committee, the Standard Operating Procedure committee, the EMS committee, and the Public Speaker's Bureau. I have been certified/qualified to drive and operate two of our Truck companies and have spent almost three years as an on-call and shift Fire Investigator/P.I.O. I have also been performing fire and life safety inspections during the annual Santa Clara County Fair for the past four years and have been a CPR instructor, and Paramedic/EMT skills instructor within the department since I was hired.

On my days off, I am employed by Chabot College in Hayward as the EMT program director and primary instructor, and also as an adjunct faculty member within the Paramedic and Fire Service Technology programs. As the EMT program director, I am responsible for scheduling, planning, budgeting, organizing, and coordinating all aspects of the EMT basic and refresher programs and also for supervising, motivating, and training a staff of 20 instructors.

I also spent 13 years with Longs Drug Stores. I mention this for two reasons. One being that I spent 3 1/2 years as a manager: ensuring optimum customer relations, and supervising, motivating, and training a staff of up to 40 employees; and the other being that they taught me a great deal about Customer Service. Longs prides themselves in their customer service, as does our great Department.

Besides this preparation, I am a dependable, motivated, loyal, and flexible person that is ready to take on the challenges of the position and continue maintaining and improving on the Values of the Department, which are customer service, diversity, integrity, teamwork, and most of all, our employees."

SUMMARY:

I have provided that information not for you to use the same opening statement for yourself, but for you to see how powerful and impacting your opening statement needs to be. I think I was able to properly set the stage for the rest of my interview and to also stick out above the other candidates, based on my opening statement.

How To Answer The Opening Statement:

There are two ways to answer an opening statement question:

1. **Categorizing**—The way I did it above, by categorizing each of my key areas of preparation—education, training, experience, and personal characteristics, and then taking the time to discuss each of them. If done properly, it makes each of them stick out and be highlighted.
2. **Chronologically**—For example, telling a story of when you were first attracted to a career in the fire service up until now. Including everything you have done to prepare yourself for a career in the fire service (education, training, experience, etc.). This way of answering an opening statement is your way of taking the oral board on a journey. Be careful though; do not take them on a journey that does not have a destination! Rambling on and on, without any structure or organization, will surely doom your score and keep you from getting the badge.

No Opportunity For Opening Statement?

What happens if you are not offered the opportunity to provide an opening statement?

Not every fire department allows candidates to provide an opening statement. Some fire department oral boards start out by asking you simulation questions or other questions that are not as open-ended as an opening statement. This requires you, the prepared candidate, to be able to think on your feet and be able to "fill in the blanks" regarding your qualifications, in each of the oral board questions. This can be very difficult to do, especially if you are not 100% familiar with the knowledge, skills, and abilities you have to offer (which should be on your resume and also the majority of your opening statement), or if you do not have your opening statement committed to memory.

If you do not adequately recognize the fact that you were not given the opportunity to provide an opening statement during the course of your interview, you stand a great chance of losing the one of the best (and only) chances to sell your knowledge, skills, and abilities and let them know why YOU are the best candidate for the position!

So here is a tip for you to remember. If the first question the oral board asks you is not one of the three typical opening statement questions that I mentioned earlier, then you have to almost believe they will not give you an opportunity to make an opening statement. There are many oral boards that don't let candidates provide an opening or closing statement; they want to hear your answers on the other questions.

I remember testing with a big-city fire department in California. They didn't want any resumes from the candidates, they didn't want the oral board to know your name, and they didn't want the candidates to have the opportunity to have an opening statement or a closing statement. They asked about six or seven questions (most of them scenario-based) and it appeared they did not want the candidates to be able to offer their knowledge, skills, and abilities to the oral board. Well then, if there are 2000 candidates interviewing for 100 positions, and you are faced with a similar situation, what are you to do?

This was a learning experience for me because I did not handle the situation as good as I could have. It was not until they had asked most of the questions that I realized that I was not going to have the chance to provide my opening statement. I had gone on answering their questions to the best of my ability (or so I had thought), without getting into much of my key selling points. I knew I was doomed when after the last scenario question, they advised me that there were no more questions and that I would find out my results in the mail. After picking up my jaw off of the ground, I thanked the oral board for their time, shook their hands, and walked out the door. I had just completed an interview, and had only provided about 10% of my knowledge, skills, and abilities to the oral panel.

What did I learn from that situation and what did I do in the future to prevent a similar situation from ever occurring again? Anytime I had an interview and the first question was a "non-opening statement question," I had to assume that there would not be an opening statement and there was a good chance there might not be a closing statement either. If that was the case, I knew I had to sprinkle in all of my experience, training and education, community service, personal characteristics, etc. (my knowledge, skills, and abilities) into EACH of the questions. This was risky because I never knew how many questions there were going to be and I also had to ensure I covered as much of background as I could over all of the questions.

So if the first question was "tell us your greatest strength," and you said "dependability," then you could maybe add one of your work experiences to this answer. For example, you could say "my greatest strength would have to be my dependability. Presently I work for XYZ plumbing in San Jose. In the ten years I have worked there, I have never called in sick, never been late to work, and never missed a day of work due to injury. I realize how much my employer depends on me to be there every day, so that his customers can have the best service they deserve. Since there are only five other plumbers in our company, having one employee off work can lead to a delay in the customers' problems solved on an expedient basis." See how I was able to sprinkle a part of my background into one question?

Then say the next question is "provide us with a time when you had to mediate a dispute?" You could answer something to the effect of "last year, while at Chabot College in Hayward—where I received my A.A. degree in Fire Technology as well as completed my EMT and Firefighter 1 academy training, I came across a situation where two students in one of my fire technology classes were almost on the verge of punching each other over the last textbook in the bookstore. Both of them felt they had gotten their hand on the book first, and neither was planning on giving it up.

The book was probably going to be ripped in half before one or the other student would have been able to purchase it. Tensions were tight since certain books can be hard to come by, and also because this was the first day of class and their instructor were very adamant about each student having their books on the first day of class. I could definitely sympathize with both students, since I had taken that class last semester. Knowing that I still had my book from last semester's class, I offered to sell my book to either student at a slightly lower price. While it is not always the safest thing to try and get into the middle of disputes, I felt that I could try this one idea that all parties would benefit from. After a little bit of convincing, the students agreed to have me flip a coin to determine who would get the book at the reduced price."

Not only was I able to answer the question, I was able to also provide something about my education (the fact that I have an A.A. degree in fire technology and that I have also completed my EMT and Firefighter 1 academy training) in a way that tied into the question.

SUMMARY:

It has been said that a candidate has about 30 seconds to make a lasting impression on the oral board, once they walk through the door, and I firmly believe that. Besides your own demeanor and body language, your oral communication skills have to be at an excellent level, and you have to be able to hit the ground running once you get asked that first question. If you cannot get the interest of your oral board in the first 30 seconds, your chances of getting a top score are very limited!

# # # #

Oral Interviews: The Closing Statement

One of the most important phases of an oral interview is the closing statement. The closing statement, if you are provided the opportunity to do one, is your last chance for you to sell yourself and the best chance for the oral board to remember you in a positive and unique way.

In some oral boards, it is not uncommon for interviews to occur for one week or more, and for hundreds of candidates to be interviewed by the same oral board panel. A firefighter candidate is getting rated during their interview and immediately after their interview concludes. Another thing that may occur after all of the candidates have been interviewed and ranked (based on their oral board scores), is that all candidates are then re-ranked, based on what the oral board can remember about each of them and based on the needs of the department. If the oral board is re-ranking candidates after the interviews have ended (and your interview occurred on the first of ten days of interviews), it is critical that you leave the oral board on a high note and with a good taste in their mouth.

Most of the candidates being interviewed have very similar backgrounds and experiences: EMT and/or paramedic training, certifications such as firefighter 1, education such as a two-year degree in fire technology and having completed a firefighter academy, volunteer experience, etc. The list goes on-and-on, and this can make it tough for candidates to stick out and be remembered after the last interview is concluded. That is why having a strong closing statement that the oral board members can correlate to you after the interviews have ended is so important.

Here is a typical closing statement question:

- That concludes all of the questions. Is there anything else you would like to add or feel that you may have left out?

How To Answer The Closing Statement:

There are three ways you can answer a closing statement:

1. You can just thank them for their time and then get up to leave (some candidates utilize this method).
2. You can just ramble on, repeat things you've already said, and sound disorganized and unprepared (most candidates utilize this method).
3. You can have a strong, powerful, jaw-dropping closing statement that has been prepared and rehearsed (very few candidates utilize this method—and I think this is the best way to handle the closing statement).

How long should a closing statement be?

In a perfect world, it should be anywhere from 30 seconds to a minute. Any more than that and you're going to bore them to death and have them contemplate reducing your overall score you have tried so hard to do your best at.

What information should your closing statement contain?

Your closing statement is not, I repeat not, an opportunity to repeat everything you have said in your opening statement and in your interview. While it can be true that people learn through repetition, and also remember things through repetition, the goals of your closing statement are to:

1. Include things you may have left out in your opening statement (important accomplishments, knowledge, skills, and/or abilities).
2. Let the oral board know that you really want the position you are applying for (surprisingly enough, many candidates fail to let the oral panel know that they really want the position they are applying for and that they really want to work for the agency they are applying for).

3. Leave the oral board wanting to hear more about you (as opposed to the opposite—their wanting you to leave the room as fast as you humanly possible).

Does every agency allow candidates to have a closing statement?

No; but it is better to be prepared to have one than not have one. If they don't allow you the opportunity to make a closing statement, you better hope you were able to cover all of the bases in your previous questions. Since some departments do not permit closing statements, this is why I feel it is important to state all of your key accomplishments, your pertinent knowledge, skills, and abilities, as well as your desire and motivation to become a member of that agency you are applying for in your opening statement and in your other questions you are answering.

When I was testing for the position of entry-level firefighter, I quickly learned I had to have a closing statement that would just drive home the fact to the oral board that I was the best candidate for the position. I also learned I would have to provide some form of "shock-value" to my interview. When I say shock-value, I mean it in a positive way. Virtually every candidate has something positive and unique to offer the fire department in the way of knowledge, skills, and / or abilities. However, most of the candidates typically do not know how to make themselves stand out and be remembered.

When I have to participate in an oral board (as an rater), I know that one of the best ways to have the oral board remember me is to have a strong opening and closing statements. I also know another way is to provide some form of "shock-value" so that they will remember me for at least the rest of the time the oral boards are in existence. Why is this so important? Well, oral boards are expected to be non-biased and objective, and are not supposed to judge one candidate to another candidate. They are supposed to objectively grade candidates against a pre-determined and standardized rating form.

Well, I think we all can agree it is virtually impossible to do this, because we all are biased in one form or another. Even if the oral board members are briefed and trained in advance to help reduce bias and subjectivity, it is still impossible for them to not be influenced by you in some form or fashion; that is human nature and something you should try to work on to go in your favor. Now providing "shock-value" is nothing that is illegal, immoral, or unethical. It is providing the oral board with information that will hopefully show them how UNIQUE you are as compared to other candidates.

For example, when I first started testing to become a firefighter, I was working full-time at a retail drug store chain. I was getting paid a decent wage (so I thought at the time) and was having fun working there. However, I soon realized it was not the career for me to continue in for the next 30 years. When I made the decision to put as much time as I could into becoming a firefighter, I knew I would probably have to go back to part-time status so that I could have more time to take tests, educate myself, go to paramedic school, perform volunteer work, etc. Going part-time was going to cost me about $20,000 per year in lost wages, but I knew it was going to be worth it in the long run.

I ended up packaging that into my closing statement as a form of "shock-value" to prove to the oral boards that I was motivated and dedicated to becoming a firefighter, and that I was willing to make sacrifices to get into the fire service.

Here is the closing statement I used when I was testing for entry-level firefighter:

"I would like to first thank the members of the oral board for your time and for allowing me to be here today. In the short time we have been together, I hope I have shown you how much I want to become a firefighter for the _____ fire department. Becoming a firefighter is something I have wanted since I was a little kid. I realize that sounds cliché, but it is true. At a young age, I was visiting fire stations on a regular basis, I was a subscriber to Firehouse magazine in it's first year of existence, I was listening to the local fire departments on my scanner, and I was talking about a career as a firefighter with a couple of family friends who had worked for the San Leandro Fire Department—one is now a captain and the other is a deputy chief. Both of those officers have helped me realize that I want a career in the fire service.

Lastly, I hope I have been able to show you all how motivated and dedicated I am to becoming a firefighter. I have been testing now for the last few years; I have been driving around the state taking firefighter examinations and participating in fire related educational and training opportunities so that I can best prepare myself for the career of my dreams. However I am ready to settle down and get on with my career. I have also made many sacrifices to become a firefighter, the biggest one being the $20,000 pay cut when I stepped down from my management position at Longs Drugs to a part-time position, so that I could have more time to take tests, further my education, and better prepare for a career in the fire service. Becoming a firefighter with the _____ fire department would be a dream come true; please give me the opportunity to work for the _____fire department and I will do my best to be an asset to the department!"

SUMMARY:

If you were on the oral board and you heard a closing statement similar to the one above, do you think you would remember the candidate? You bet you would. Would that closing statement help you stand out above the other candidates? You bet it would. Shortly after I mentioned that I took a $20,000 a year pay cut to better prepare myself for a career in the fire service, it was not uncommon to see the jaws of the oral board members hit the table (or so it appeared) and see them start smiling and showing some enthusiasm! Why would they act this way? Partly because they could maybe relate and/or appreciate what I was doing, partly because I had maybe shown them truly how motivated and dedicated I was at becoming a firefighter, and partly because they had probably not heard many great closing statements in their time on the panel.

Think about that. The same oral board is interviewing candidates for two weeks straight, for eight hours each day, and seeing new candidates every 30 minutes. Is it tough for the oral board to remain focused and motivated? Of course it is. Besides being hard work for them to have to sit and stay focused and objective, it doesn't help when the majority of the candidates come through their panel sounding like each other (clone answers, unenthusiastic, boring, unprepared, unmotivated, unable to validate what they say, unorganized, etc.). Do what you can to be the candidate that is the one that stands out for the day (and the entire length of the panel) so that you make them compare you against the other candidates.

Here is the closing statement I used when I took the captain's test:

"First of all, I would like to thank you, the members of the board, for your time and your effort. Second, I hope I have been able to show that I have the knowledge, skills, and abilities for the position of Fire Captain and how my education, training, and experience have prepared me for the position of Fire Captain. Something I have believe that sets me apart from the other well qualified candidates is my motivation, dedication, desire, and most of all, enthusiasm in becoming a Fire Captain for this great Department. A promotion to Fire Captain would be a dream come true for me.

My preparation began even before I was hired here as an entry-level Firefighter/Engineer. I figure I have spent over 1500 hours taking classes anywhere throughout the state from Chico down to San Bernardino. While the department pays for the tuition, I have spent thousands of dollars, out of my own pocket, on motel rooms, have driven thousands of miles in my car, and have spent countless hours away from my wife (I'm very lucky that she supports me 100% and also works in the fire service). All of this just to prepare me to be the best fire officer I can be. I have made a lot of sacrifices to get where I am at today.

Give me the chance and you can count on me to continue my motivation, dedication, desire, and enthusiasm to the fire service, to the community, to the Department, and to the position of Fire Captain. When the going gets tough, I plan to be the Captain that my Battalion Chief has to worry about the least. I have prepared myself to be the best that I can be so that I can provide the best possible service to the members of the department and the citizens that are served by the our Department. Thank you very much!"

SUMMARY:

The closing statement above must have worked; I scored 100% on the oral interview and came out number one in the assessment center!
The key thing to remember about the closing statement is that you want to leave the board wanting to hear more and to have them smiling and talking about you (in a positive way) after you have left the room. Correlate a closing statement to the music world. When a band has finished their main set, they say goodbye to the audience and the lights go down. "San Jose—you've been great! We'll see you soon! At this point, the lights go down and the audience will usually start clapping for an encore (typically one, two, or three additional songs). If you have ever been to a concert, you can appreciate the energy in the air when the band is ready to do an encore and when they have finished their encore. If the band did their job, you left the concert feeling great and with a very positive feeling of the band, and you usually talk about the concert the next day at work or at school to your friends. This is no different from someone in an oral board.

The oral board wants everyone to succeed and they want to hear and see everyone at their best. However, since nobody is perfect, the oral board usually sees people from their best to their worst; and most people are at their average. Use the closing statement to your advantage and strive to be one of those candidates that the oral board is talking about for days after the interview (in a positive way—there are enough candidates oral board members talk about that were not at their best performance level—try not to fall in that category). Take the time to write out your closing statement and to put it on your computer (just like I suggested doing with your opening statement). That way you can modify it as necessary and also print it out to review with your opening statement while you are waiting to be called in to the oral board. Most candidates come across as average candidates—that is why it is so critical for you to have a strong closing statement; it is an additional tool for you to use when you are in an oral board interview to help score the most points you can so that you don't have to take another entry-level test in your career!

Oral Interview Tip #1: Don't Just Answer The Question, Answer The Question!

Many firefighter candidates do not take the time to completely answer the question they are asked in an oral interview. They answer the question with enough information to receive a passing score, but not enough information to receive the best possible score. There is a way you can answer the question in a detailed way, without sounding like you are rambling on and on. This is why I say, "don't just answer the question, answer the question!"

Let's look at a simple question that is asked at many entry-level interviews, "what is your greatest strength?" There really is not one right answer for that question. Any strength you think of can provide you with the highest possible score for that question, assuming you don't just answer the question, and that you answer the question! Now it is a good rule of thumb to have an answer that is unique to you and does not sound like a typical clone answer that the majority of candidates have used in their interview, prior to your sitting in the hot seat.

Let's get back to the original question, "what is your greatest strength?" The immediate response that comes to your head is to tell the oral board that you are loyal. While being loyal can be considered to be a clone answer, the response itself would provide the candidate with a passing score. Notice I didn't say an above average or an excellent score for that question. I said a passing score. In school, C's and D's are passing. B's are above average and A's are excellent scores. When a fire department is interviewing hundreds if not thousands of candidates, who do you think gets the job offer, the candidate receiving the "passing score" or the candidate with the "excellent score?" I think the answer is obvious.

How do you make that answer of "I am loyal" into an "excellent score" you may wonder? Do I need to respond with another answer that doesn't sound like a clone answer? That is one way, but not the primary way. The primary way is to be a little more detailed in your response and to also provide an example.

Key point: every time you state something, such as I am dedicated, I am loyal, I am motivated, I get along well with others, always make sure you state an example to prove to the oral board why it is that you are dedicated, loyal, motivated, etc.

Now if you took the time and effort to answer that question with an answer of "my greatest strength would have to be that I am loyal. I have worked for the same employer for the last ten years. I have had numerous job opportunities I could have taken, many of which could have provided me more money and better benefits; however, because of my present employer's flexibility with my scheduling so I could obtain my fire technology degree and also take as many firefighter tests that I qualified for, I have felt an obligation to work there until I obtained the career of my dreams, one of being a firefighter. Their understanding of my wanting to become a firefighter while knowing that I was planning on eventually leaving their company was something that could have been looked upon very negatively by them. Because of their loyalty to me, I feel it is my duty and obligation to be loyal to them as well. Since firefighters are expected to be loyal to their department, community and fellow firefighters, I feel my greatest strength of being loyal is something that will be an asset to the (insert the name of the department you are testing for) Fire Department."

Doesn't that answer sound better than just stating, "I am loyal," or "my greatest strength is that I am loyal?" Be careful with providing too much detail because it can come across as rambling, causing the oral board to miss your point and start wondering to themselves, "when does this story end," or "where is this story going?"

Providing an example helps make a clone answer turn into an answer that is more detailed, but more importantly, an answer that provides a detailed fact or reason why the oral panel should believe what you are saying. Providing an example will help turn a passing score for that question into an above average or excellent score. Everybody says things about themselves. However, not many candidates take the time to actually "put their money where their mouth is" and prove to the oral panel why they are what they say they are.

Anyone can throw words out there to sound impressive. The successful candidates also add some detail to those words and provide an example to every statement to help validate and provide credibility to what they are attempting to convey to the oral board. Think of the concept every time you are asked a question in an oral interview and you should start to see your scores increasing!

# # # #

Oral Interview Tip #2: Increase Your Oral Interview Scores With The "Introduction—Body— Conclusion" Concept

It is safe to say that the oral interview is the most important and most critical phase of the firefighter testing process. You can be the most physically fit individual, have the highest written test score, and have the best resume when compared to all of the other candidates, but if you cannot successfully sell yourself during the oral interview, you will never get a chance to become a firefighter. Most fire departments usually score the oral interview as 100% of your overall score, which translates to your final ranking on the eligibility list. If you cannot effectively communicate your knowledge, skills, and abilities to the oral interview panel, you will not get the job!

Most candidates are able to get a passing score on the oral interview. When I say passing, I mean at least 70%. Yes, there will always be some that don't make the minimum score (which is usually 70%) to continue in the hiring process. Additionally, there will always be a small percentage (usually less than 10% of all of the candidates being interviewed) that are able to score in the high 90 percentile; high enough to get to the Chief's interview and eventually get the job. However, most candidates will probably score in the 70 to 80 percentile; good enough to pass the oral interview, but not good enough to be considered any further in the hiring process.

What makes a score in the 90 percentile? What makes an answer to an oral board question better than the other ones the oral board has been hearing? What differentiates an excellent answer to just a good answer? Those are all questions I plan to answer for you.

In the previous section, I discussed the concept of "Don't just answer the question, answer the question!" What I was trying to get across was that with a little bit of effort, you can add some points to your overall score by being more-detailed (not rambling, but more-detailed and more thorough when answering oral board questions). In addition to that method, I want to introduce another concept that I think can also add some points to your overall score, putting you closer to that perfect score of 100%. This concept I like to call "Intro-body-conclusion," and it can be used any time you answer a question!

In my experience, when asked a question, most candidates go straight to the answer, without having set the stage or warmed up the panel members. Excellent athletes warm up before they play their game. Good musicians warm up before they go on stage. Excellent public speakers warm up their audience before they get into the "meat of the matter" or their best subject material.

Let me give you an example. You are asked the question, what is your greatest strength? Most candidates would provide an answer by going right to the point. They would either reply something to the effect of "I'm dependable," "dependability," or "I would have to say my greatest strength is my dependability." Answering a question with any of the above responses would get you a score of somewhere in the 70 to 80 percentiles. Let's not even get into the fact that using an answer such as "dependable" could be considered using a clone answer (an answer many other people are using. While that is true, work with me while I use it as an example).

Remember what I talked about regarding "don't just answer the question, answer the question." Providing more detail (and a specific example) will help increase that score of 70 to 80% up into the high 80's or maybe even the 90's. So now you answer that same question—what is your greatest strength?—"I would have to say dependability, because I have been working at the same company, Starbucks, for the past seven years and have not called in sick once." Providing a real-life example and being more detailed just gave you a few more points. Enough points to get to the Fire Chief's interview and eventually get the job? Maybe; maybe not.

How do I then increase my score even higher, and get one of the top oral board scores? By following the "intro-body-conclusion" concept.

Put yourself into a classroom for a minute. If you had a teacher ask you to write a term paper or research paper, would you go straight to the story? No! You would first start out by writing an introduction (maybe a paragraph), then by going into your body (your outline; a couple of bullet points that you are going to expand on), and then by finishing it up with a summary or conclusion (maybe a paragraph). Thus, the name "intro-body-conclusion." Without properly setting the stage for what you are going to be talking about, or even wrapping everything up in the end, the reader is left in the dark about why this is important for them to read, what it is they are going to get out of reading your paper, and what your key points were.

When I was in my first instructor training class, I remember hearing the instructor tell us a method that good instructors use when presenting material. He told us you first have to "tell them what you're going to tell them," you then need to "tell them," and then you need to "tell them what you told them." The "tell them what you're going to tell them" is your introduction, the "tell them" is your body, and the "tell them what you told them" is your conclusion.

Take that same method and apply it to public speaking (which is what you are doing in an oral interview). Excellent speakers don't just start talking about their main topics. They always attempt to warm-up the audience with some jokes or some other material that will set the stage for what they are going to talk about (I usually don't advocate using jokes in a fire service oral interview). Two of the best late night television hosts, Jay Leno and Dave Letterman are good examples of this. For about the first five or so minutes of their show, they take the time to warm up their audience by telling jokes, to get them ready and excited for their main show. They are motivating the audience to get them ready for what they really want to cover that night. Consider that the "introduction."

I have been to many rock concerts over my lifetime and this concept is also applied in this arena as well. The audience usually knows when the headlining act is getting to hit the stage. The lights go down. There is usually some form of entrance music playing. Then, the announcer gets on the microphone "Oakland California, you've wanted the best, you've got the best . . . . the hottest band in the world, KISS!!!!!" The audience goes nuts. The audience is motivated and standing up, watching the performance and focusing on the performers. Consider that the "introduction."

Think of the above items in the same fashion as you would your introduction while beginning to answer your oral board question.

As for the body of your answer, I'm not really going to discuss that at this point because I think most of us have no problem coming up with an answer to a question. Some answer the body with a simple answer; some provide a more detailed answer.

Now, for the conclusion of your oral board answer to a question: You've given an introduction. You've talked in detail (and did not ramble on-and-on or go off in any tangents), and now it is time to bring this question to a close. Think back to when you had to write that term paper. This is your conclusion, your summary, your chance to bring everything to a close, your chance to reiterate your key points and end this question so you can go on to the next one. How can I successfully wrap this question up and sound organized and well spoken?

Every good thing must come to an end. Every good speaker summarizes their body of their speech and finishes up with some words that leave the audience wanting more and remembering what it was they came to hear. Every good musician / band leaves the stage with at least one song as an encore and with thanking the audience for coming there, leaving the audience wanting more. Consider this their conclusion.

Answering On Oral Board Question:

Now let's look at the same question, "what is your greatest strength," and attempt to answer it using the "intro-body-conclusion" concept. Let's dissect it piece-by-piece.

Intro:
___

"While I believe I have many strengths that can relate to the fire service, let me concentrate on my dependability and how it relates to the fire service."

Body:
___

"Dependability is not only my greatest strength, but also one of my core values. I pride myself in being dependable. For example, I have been working at Safeway Stores for the last seven years now, and I have never called in sick or missed one day of work because of injury or illness. I make it a point to keep myself healthy and also realize that people are counting on me in some form or fashion, so I do what I have to do to make sure I am dependable, whatever the situation is."

Conclusion:

"Dependability is one of the greatest strengths a firefighter can have. Whether it is showing up to work on time to relieve the person going off duty, following through on orders given to me by a superior officer, or working as a part of the team either on the fireground or around the fire station, being dependable is one of the most critical traits a firefighter can possess, and I believe I can bring that strength to the (include the name of the fire department you are testing for)."

That may seem to be a long-winded answer, as opposed to just stating a one-word or one sentence answer. However, does it not sound a bit more organized, detailed, thorough, and complete?

While I imagine there may be a couple of oral board questions that can be answered with a simple one-word answer (such as yes or no), I believe you can use the intro-body-conclusion format when answering any question, and make yourself sound more organized, and also help you stand out when compared to the other candidates.

When testing with hundreds if not thousands of other candidates, it is paramount to stand out in a positive and unique way. Answering your oral board questions using the intro-body-conclusion method will help you stand out in a positive and unique way, while also making you sound professional and organized. You only get one opportunity at the oral interview; properly prepare yourself and answer the questions with the "intro-body-conclusion" concept and you should see your scores increase drastically.

# # # #

What Not To Do During An Oral Interview

Just like there are a lot of things to do during an interview, there are a number of things to NOT do during an interview . . .

A survey found in the newspaper USA Today on June 7, 2013 on page A1 asked the following question related to job candidates in the age range of 18 to 24 years of age: "What are the biggest mistakes young job candidates make during an interview?"

The answers were as follows:

- Inappropriate attire   = 50%
- Being late or at the wrong time/date   = 44%
- Overly aggressive about job expectations   = 36%
- Lack of eye contact   = 33%
- Checking phone/texting   = 30%

Really? You may be surprised and say those things don't occur. Well, I've been a rater and proctor on enough oral interviews to say I've actually seen a number of those things occur, even in the fire service. Chances are as time goes on, we'll only see more of the above occurring because of the perceived lack of social skills that seems to be very rampant and evident in the younger generations today. Who are the future older generations? The current younger generations of course. It's hard to teach an old dog new tricks, and we are all creatures of habit.

What does this mean for you? Learn from the mistakes of others to allow yourself to not make the same mistakes and instead stand above your competition!

# # # #

Most Common Oral Interview Questions

Most departments today utilize what is known as a structured oral interview. In a structured oral interview, the oral panel asks all of the candidates the same questions. They have a pre-designated, standardized list of questions to ensure all candidates are being asked the same question, to help ensure reliability during the testing process. If they asked different questions to different candidates, it would be difficult to be able to grade each of the candidates similarly, thus raising questions of how reliable the test actually is.

Typical oral interview questions an oral board may ask you are:

1. Tell us about yourself. (An opening statement question).
2. Tell us how your education, experience, and training has prepared you for a career in the fire service. (An opening statement question).
3. Tell us how you have prepared yourself to become a firefighter. (An opening statement question).
4. Tell us why you want to be a firefighter.
5. Tell us why you want to work for our fire department.
6. Tell us what you know about our fire department.
7. Tell us what you know about our city (or county, or area that we provide services to).
8. Tell us what your greatest strength is.
9. Tell us what your greatest weakness is and what you are doing to improve that weakness.
10. Tell us your definition of customer service and why it is important to the fire service.
11. Tell us your definition of cultural diversity and why it is important to the fire service.
12. Tell us what you think is the daily routine of a firefighter for our department.
13. Tell us what you think is the biggest challenge facing the fire service today.

14. Tell us what you think is the biggest challenge facing this department today or in the future.
15. That concludes all of the questions. Is there anything you left out or would like to add? (A closing statement).

Before you answer an oral board question, remember these tips to help you get the best score you can get on each of the questions:

1. **Listen to the entire question.**

   There is nothing worse than having to ask the oral board to repeat the question. It shows you have poor listening skills. If all else fails, you can ask the oral board to repeat the question, but try not to get into the habit of doing that. Firefighters need to have excellent listening skills, and this is one of the main times you will be evaluated for such.

2. **Don't immediately blurt out your answer.**

   Take a second to process the question asked of you, pause for a second (as opposed to saying a filler word such as uhm or ah) and then provide your answer.

3. **Make sure you answer the entire question.**

   Sometimes an oral board will ask you a two-part or three-part question (multiple questions within the one answer); answering only one of the parts will result in your losing up to half (or more) of the possible points on that question.

4. **Try to stay away from simple, one or two-word answers.**

   If at all possible, try to have an answer that sounds well organized and thought out. If you state a fact, or perceived fact (such as "I am dependable"), always back it up with an example; that will help validate your answer. Telling the board you are dependable doesn't hold much weight. Telling the board you are dependable because you have worked at the same job for five years and have not called in sick one day shows the board that you are dependable.

5. **If you don't know the answer to a question, don't try to fake it or bluff your way through it.**

Doing so will definitely show and also put you in jeopardy of losing credibility and/or valuable points. There is nothing wrong with saying "I don't know." There is something wrong with trying to B.S. the oral board; nobody wants to work with a liar or someone that always thinks they know it all. However, be careful of having to say "I don't know" too many times. Once is ok. Saying it a few times (or more) shows that you're not prepared and that you better do some research before your next interview.

# # # #

Additional Oral Interview Questions

Candidates need to prepared for virtually any type of question that is asked of them. I honestly believe there are no such thing as "trick questions." If a question catches you by surprise, it means you didn't adequately prepare for all of the different types of questions you may be asked. In addition to the questions above, take some time to review all of the questions on the following pages and attempt to formulate possible answers should they ever be asked of you.

General Questions:

1. Tell us about yourself.
2. Tell us how your education, training and experience has prepared you to become a firefighter?
3. What have you done personally and professionally to prepare yourself to become a firefighter?
4. What are three personal attributes that will make you a successful firefighter?
5. What is cultural diversity and how does it apply to the fire service?
6. Why is cultural diversity important for the fire service and this fire department?
7. Describe a time when you had to resolve a conflict.
8. What is customer service and how does it apply to the fire department?
9. Give us an example of when you have provided "outstanding" customer service.
10. What is your greatest fear, and how do you handle it?
11. Is there any order you would disobey from your captain?
12. How are you involved in your community?
13. Please tell us your current and past history of performing community service?
14. What can you contribute to our fire department?
15. How would you describe the concept of discipline?

16. Why do you believe you would be a good firefighter?
17. Why do you want to be a firefighter?
18. What did you do to prepare for this interview?
19. How would you keep physically fit after being hired?
20. How would you deal with the boredom and stress of this job?
21. How would you deal with working 24 hour shifts with various people?
22. What do you see as the positive and negative aspects of being a firefighter?
23. How do you feel about telling a mother that her child has died?
24. How do you feel about receiving an order to improve your personal hygiene?
25. What experiences have you had working as a team member?
26. What improvement in a past job have you made?
27. What should we hire you over the other candidates?
28. What does a firefighter's day involve other than firefighting?
29. If we hire you, do you intend to spend your entire career in this department?
30. What is your ultimate goal in the fire service?
31. What are you looking for in a career as a firefighter?
32. What is the most important feature you can bring to this fire department?
33. How do you feel about wearing a uniform?
34. How do you feel about HIV and other communicable diseases you may be exposed to on the job?
35. If we hire you, and another department calls you for a job, will you leave our department for that department?
36. How do you feel about working with women?
37. What are the differences between a large and a small fire department?
38. Tell us what your biggest accomplishment in your life has been so far?
39. If you had a choice, who would you work with, a female, a white male, or a black male? What would be the basis for your decision?

40. How does your current job relate to the fire service?
41. What was the best/worst job you have ever had, and why was it the best/worst?
42. What are some of the sacrifices you will have to make to have a career in the fire service?
43. What are the three most important things that have prepared you for the fire service?
44. If you are selected as a firefighter for our department, what can we expect you to do for us and what will you expect the department to do for you?
45. Why does tension develop in the fire house? What can you offer to minimize such tensions?
46. Why does the fire service try to instill a sense of teamwork among its members?
47. Should a fire department be able to dictate a no-smoking policy to its members? How about an off-duty no-smoking policy? Why or why not?
48. What is your greatest strength and your greatest weakness? Regarding the weakness, what are you doing to improve upon it?
49. Do you have any questions of the Board?
50. That concludes all of the questions. Do you have anything you may have left out or want to add?

EMT Questions

1. What is a pneumothorax and how would you treat it?
2. You respond to an accident with a 25-year-old male with a suspected cervical spine injury. How would you handle the situation?
3. You get called to an overdose. When you get there you find out it's your best friend. The day before, he told you that he just bought some marijuana and he hid it in his garage. What are you going to do?
4. What is triage and when do you use it?

5. What are the signs and symptoms of a heart attack?

6. Please tell us the signs and symptoms of heat exhaustion versus heat stroke.

7. How would you deal with a death of a close friend on an EMS call?

8. Describe the three stages of pregnancy.

9. You respond to an EMS call where a 10-year-old boy is cyanotic. What would you do for this person?

10. Name the areas where you can take a pulse on the body.

11. What are the nine types of shock and give a brief description of each.

12. What are the different layers of skin?

13. Name the five types of wounds.

14. What kind of drug would cause pinpoint pupils?

15. What is gastric distention?

16. You respond to an auto accident versus a tree. There are two persons inside the car and one of the victims hit his head on the windshield. Both victims are unconscious. What would the actions of your engine company be?

17. You respond to a head-on vehicle accident with one person still inside the car and one person thrown out of the car face down. What would the actions of your engine company be?

18. You respond to an EMS call and a 13-year-old female has committed suicide. How would you confront her parents?

19. You receive a call for a vehicle accident. The car crashed into a tree and the female in the car is lying with her head against the dash, with no vital signs. What do you think your captain will order you to do?

Situational Questions

1. You respond to an overturned gasoline tanker truck with a patient still inside the cab. Your captain wants you and the other firefighter to extricate this person. From a previous hazardous materials course, you know for a fact that this

tanker is going to explode, in other words—BLEVE. What are you going to do?

2. You are a probationary firefighter and assigned to inspect a building. Your captain sends you to the back of the building to do an inspection. When you get back there, you find a man cleaning a motorcycle with a large container of gasoline next to him. You proceed to tell him it is a violation and he curses at you and tells you to beat it. What would you do?

3. You are a probationary firefighter on a ski trip. While skiing, you see another firefighter who should be working but called in sick so he could go skiing. What would you do?

4. You respond to a fully involved structure fire in a house; the owner comes up to you and tells you that there is a victim still inside that needs to be rescued. He tells you to follow him so he can show you where the person is. What would you do?

5. You are on a call and one of your fellow firefighters gets seriously injured. How would you deal with the situation?

6. As a firefighter, you and your captain enter a burning building. As you enter the structure, you notice two unconscious people in the hallway. At this point, your captain collapses. What would you do?

7. You are a firefighter assigned to do an inspection of a small business. You find a major violation while doing the inspection. How are you going to approach the owner and explain it to him/her?

8. You have just started your probationary period and while doing overhaul on the fireground one day, you feel a strong sharp pain down your lower back and left leg. No one has noticed. What are you going to do?

9. You are a probationary firefighter and you see your shift captain filling his car up with gas at the corporation yard. What would you do?

10. You are a probationary firefighter and when you get ready for bed, someone has taken the bed that your captain has assigned to you. What would you do?

11. You are a probationary firefighter and are taking a test. You notice other probationary firefighters cheating. What would you do?

12. You arrive on scene of an auto versus auto accident; upon examination of one of the patients, you find him breathing but with no pulse. What would you do?

13. You are a probationary firefighter, and you and your captain enter a burning building; shortly after entering, you feel the structure is unsafe. What would you do?

14. You are on an engine company, and are responding to an EMS call. When you come back to the engine from inside the house, the engine is gone. What would you do?

15. You notice a fellow firefighter who is on duty drinking at a chili cook off function. What would you do?

16. What do you do when you come to work on your first day and another firefighter sprays you with a fire extinguisher and your uniform becomes dirty? What would you do? Second part of the question: You have a talk with him after he does this two more times. What would you do?

17. Suppose you witness another firefighter backing a fire truck into a utility pole. This causes the rungs of the aerial ladder to be bent, damaging the ladder. The firefighter does not see you and continues to maneuver the truck as if nothing happened. What would you do and why?

18. What would you do if you suspected a fellow firefighter is having a drug problem?

19. You notice that someone is eating your food out of the refrigerator while you are on shift. What would you do and why?

20. While you and your co-workers are attending to a small trash fire at which a group has gathered, a person begins to verbally abuse you. What would you do and why?

21. It is a fire department rule that no alcoholic beverages can be consumed within the fire station. As you are cleaning the fire station one day, you notice a bottle of alcohol under a firefighter's bed. What would you do and why?

22. At the scene of a fire at the rear of a building, the captain sends you to the front to get two SCBA bottles. On the way, a citizen asks you to please help her close her windows as the smoke is getting into her home. This would only take a few minutes. What would you do and why?

23. You are a probationary firefighter and you are studying in the dormitory when another firefighter who has been on the department 3 years comes in and turns the radio on loud enough to bother you. What would you do?

24. You and your company have just finished fighting a fire in a grocery store. As you are leaving, you see another firefighter pick up a couple of candy bars and put them into his pocket. What would you do?

25. You find two firefighters behind the fire station about ready to fight. They have been on each other's case for the last month. What would you do?

26. You are the only person at the fire station and are assigned by your captain your station duties that have to be completed in one day. However, the Mayor comes by the station with a group of citizens requesting a tour of the station. What choice of the two would you make and why?

27. You arrive on the scene of a reported structure fire and you observe a yellow-gray colored smoke puffing out of the windowsills and the doorways even though they are closed. What condition would this be and what would you do to handle this situation?

28. You are on an inspection of a small business and you find the business having 8 violations. The owner of the business becomes irate when you tell him of the violations. How would you handle the owner and convince him to get those violations corrected?

29. Your captain asks you to cut your hair. You feel it is within regulations. How are you going to handle the situation?

30. Your engine company arrives on a fire scene and your captain tells you to ladder the roof and begin ventilating. A truck captain

ladders the roof and tells you to turn off utilities. What are you going to do?

31. You arrive at 0730 hours every morning before shift starts at 0800 and make yourself orange juice for the day. Someone is continuously drinking it and you hardly get any. How would you handle the situation?

32. You see your engineer back into the chief's car, and he tells you not to say anything about the incident because he had been warned not to back the engine without a spotter. What are you going to do?

33. You are on the fireground taking care of a task on the opposite side of the building; when you return, nobody is to be seen at the engine or anywhere else. All you see are hose lines. What do you do?

34. You are told by your captain to stay in a specific spot at the fire with a hose line; he also told you why. A few minutes have gone by and another firefighter comes over and tells you to go elsewhere. What do you do?

35. What would you do if you found out someone used your uniform shirt and left it soiled at the bottom of your locker and you were going to have to use it on your next shift?

36. You and a fellow firefighter are in a house during the overhaul stage and you see him pick up a watch and put it in his coat pocket. Later, a complaint is filed because a watch is missing from that same house. What would you do?

37. It is about 12 midnight and you get out of bed to get a glass of water in the kitchen. When you get up, you just happen to see your engineer taking a drink out of a brown paper bag. What do you do?

38. You pull up to the scene of an auto accident; as you approach the vehicle, you smell a strange odor coming from the rear of the overturned big rig. What are you going to do?

39. You pull up to the scene of a structure fire and your captain jumps off the engine and runs straight for the fire without an SCBA. What are you going to do?

40. You are in your station having lunch with your crew. The doorbell rings and you and the other firefighter answer the door. As soon as you open the door, a woman begins screaming and yelling at you. She claims that the fire engine almost ran her off the road earlier that day. What are you going to say to her?
41. You are out jogging with a fellow firefighter before work. He sprains his ankle, but goes to work anyways. At work, he claims he sprained his ankle there. What are you going to do?

Firefighter 1 Questions:

1. What are the different classes of fire, their symbols, and colors?
2. What is size-up?
3. What part of firefighting is most important—fire suppression or fire prevention?
4. When should ventilation be performed?
5. What are the different methods to perform ventilation at a fire?
6. What is a parapet?
7. What is nozzle reaction?
8. What are the different hydrant color markings & what is the GPM for each of those?
9. Where should you ventilate a structure fire in relation to the fire?
10. In what areas in the job of a firefighter do you need to improve yourself? How have you compensated for this weakness or deficiency?
11. Under ICS, what positions make up the "Command Staff?"
12. Under ICS, what positions make up the "General Staff?"
13. Under ICS, what are some examples of pre-designated "facilities?"
14. Under ICS, what is the difference between a Division, a Group, and a Branch?
15. What does the term "RECEOVS" stand for?
16. What is the difference between, Strategy, Tactics, and Tasks?
17. What does LCES stand for?
18. How many classifications of Standpipe Systems are there?

19. What are the different colors of markings on sprinkler heads?
20. What are the different types of smoke alarms / detectors?
21. If you were assigned to do a business fire prevention inspection, what tools / equipment would you bring with you?
22. What constitutes "Full PPE?"

# # # #

Advice From An Oral Board Rater

The following comes from a friend of mine who wanted me to share his experiences from a recent oral board process he sat on for his department:

Hello Steve, Bob Hopken here. I am e-mailing to advise you of something that you already know I am sure but I found it to be interesting. I just served on our oral boards for our new firefighter candidates for ACFD. I have not done that for approximately 5 years because of my involvement in our academies. Anyhow, over the course of the six days of interviews, my panel saw approximately 50-60 candidates come through, many well qualified on paper, well dressed etc. However what amazed me was that approximately 75-80% of the applicants did not make any station visits or talk to ACFD personnel about coming to work there. When asked, "what do you know about ACFD and why do you want to work here," they would predominately regurgitate ACFD web based info and in essence put our panel to sleep.

Why am I sharing this? Because I wanted to give you feedback because I believe that you and Bob and the Chabot staff are doing a great job and training our next generation and I felt that I could share with you "what was missing most". What it did often times is create a clear separation . . . . some individuals appeared well qualified and could have been considered for a Chiefs interview . . . . *but this was a missing link* . . . . Station visits and truly learning about the organization in person. Hope this is helpful!

Respectfully,
Bob Hopken, ACFD Captain

# # # #

My Reflections As An Oral Board Rater

I have been fortunate to serve as an oral board candidate, an oral board rater, and an oral board proctor for a number of different departments and ranks during the years I have been in the fire service. After one of our oral boards a few years ago, I took the time to offer some feedback to candidates since I always get a lot of questions after oral boards and I wanted to offer a consistent message that I could share with all who were interested.

To set the stage, I was one of the three raters on our department oral interviews for entry-level Firefighter/Engineers assigned to paramedic duty. We had 96 candidates scheduled over an eight-day period. 12 candidates per day, starting at 0800 hours and ending at approximately 1700 hours each day. By the time of the oral interview, candidates were required to show proof of completion of the Candidate Physical Ability Test (CPAT). There were a few no shows and some that had called stating that they were not able to provide a CPAT card by their interview time.

Just some comments on the CPAT, before I go on to the oral interviews. Many candidates waited until the absolute last minute to locate and then attempt and pass the CPAT exam. This resulted in some candidates failing it the first time and not having ample time to actually retake it, and some candidates just not finding a time and place to take the CPAT that worked into their schedule. This dropped the numbers we interviewed into the high 80's if I remember correctly.

What Is The Moral Of The Story Regarding The CPAT?

1. If you have never taken it before, do so a.s.a.p. so that you know you can pass it and so you can get the certificate that most departments accept for one year.
2. If you don't know where to take the CPAT, please visit the California Professional Firefighters (CPF) website section on the CPAT at http://www.cpatonline.org to view more information including locations to take the test. If you live outside of California, start out by doing an Internet search.

3. Do attend the voluntary practice sessions, do review the informational material that is out there regarding each event, and do allow yourself ample time to retake it should you fail the first time (yes, I know we have to be positive, but we also have to have a plan b, just in case). I have heard that many of the candidates who failed it had not attended the practice sessions, something to consider.

4. Realize that just because you pass the CPAT, it doesn't mean you are in the best shape you could be in or that you could pass any physical ability test being currently offered (other than the CPAT). The CPAT is a baseline test that tells you that you are at an acceptable level of physical fitness to perform the job of a firefighter. There are some fire departments that do not use the CPAT and have tougher physical ability tests.

Now back to the oral interviews.

We had two oral interview panels set up, one to interview people with EMT certifications and the other to interview people with paramedic licenses, or that had the ability to obtain a paramedic license by time of appointment (time of job offer). We interviewed twice as many paramedics as we did EMT's, since the majority of our vacancies will probably require paramedic licensure. Here is a reason why having your paramedic license can help reduce your competition: we interviewed almost every paramedic that had applied, had passed the written examination, and had passed the CPAT. However for positions requiring EMT certification, we randomly selected about 20% of the EMT's that had applied, had passed the written examination, and had passed the CPAT.

Now being a paramedic certainly reduces your competition and definitely allows you to apply for more firefighter positions, but contrary to what some may think, it does not guarantee you a job.

The oral interview panel I sat on consisted of me (while I was still a captain), one of our battalion chiefs, and one of our firefighter/engineers assigned to paramedic duty. The three of us had a very challenging and

155

difficult task—to recommend to the fire chief the candidates that we felt would best represent the department and also fit into the department culture, based on a number of different things, most notably how well they performed in the oral interview.

We asked a total of six questions, provided the candidates 30 minutes to answer all of the questions, and then had to make a decision on whether we felt someone would make a successful firefighter for the next 30 years. Choose right and we have an excellent employee we can feel proud to have had a part in for the next 30 years. Choose wrong and there is the potential that we will be stuck with this person for the next 30 years (assuming they pass probation). Department members and we will either be proud or ashamed of the recommendations we make, all based on a 30-minute (or less) interview. Not an easy task.

While I am not able to provide specific feedback to each candidate for confidentiality reasons, I am able to provide general thoughts and comments that I think everyone who either took the interview or will be taking a fire department interview somewhere in the world in the near future will surely benefit from. The bottom line is that we make recommendations to the fire chief, but it is ultimately the fire chief's decision to hire someone in our department (in other departments, it can be a higher authority such as the city council, the city manager, the mayor, the board of supervisors, or the board of fire commissioners, just to name a few).

The last thing we want to do is to tell a specific candidate that they did an awesome job and then have the fire chief not decide to hire them for some reason. That would potentially open us up to lawsuits and inquiries that we do not need to go through. I know this sounds harsh, but the fire department you are testing for does not owe you a job; you are not entitled to a position, just because you tested and either you felt you did well, you feel you would be a good fit, or because someone said you had a great interview.

I tell all candidates the same thing—do your best in the testing process for each department and what is meant to be is meant to be. When the stars line up and your time is right, you will be offered the job. The job offer may not come from the department that you most want to work for or think you did the best at during the testing process; it may come when you least expect it. Also, just because you weren't selected for our department (or any department), don't take it personal. It wasn't meant to be. Should you take our test again, then it may be the right time. Or, I hate to say it, but it may never be the right time with our department. But don't despair, it doesn't mean that you aren't meant for another department somewhere else.

I truly believe there is a department out there for everybody. The key is to not give up and continue trying your best until you find that department.

Here are some general / specific thoughts that I wanted to share with you, based on my observations and experiences of ALL of the candidates. Think of this list as the good, the bad, and the ugly, so to speak. Try to learn from the good and the not so good of others, and realize that most of the things I mentioned were done by at least one person, some by many.

Resumes:
_____

- **Before we go any further, realize that the main difference between the resume and the job application is that the department tells you what to put on the application (usually everything) and you put what you want on the resume.** The resume is a short and sweet, to the point snapshot of who you are and what you have to offer.
- **Don't put your picture on it**. One, it can potentially go against you negatively (that dreaded d-word, discrimination); two, it just isn't cool.
- **Keep it short and sweet, easy to read, easy to follow**. We have less than a minute or so to even look at it. If things are very wordy and do not jump out at us, we're probably going to miss them.
- **Keep it to one page**. I saw two page resumes, and even one five pager. Hello, we don't have time to read all that info and it takes up space. If you're having trouble getting it down to one page, here are my suggestions:

o **You don't have to list EVERY job you've held, like you do on the application.** Include two or three of the most relevant ones, including your current one. Also, nothing says you have to list your duties on the resume; they can take up four or more lines per job. Each job should have no more than two lines each—enough room for the employer name, city/state of the employer, dates employed, and the job titles you've held.

o **Leave off your hobbies.** You're not getting hired for your hobbies, and depending on what they are, they can be looked at negatively and as a liability (i.e., drag car racer, motorcycle racer, bungee jumper, you know what I'm getting at). You're getting hired for your knowledge, skills and abilities—in a nutshell, your education, experience, training, and community service for the most part. Nothing says you can't talk about your hobbies during the interview; just don't waste valuable space on the resume.

o **Leave off any trace of high school related information.** That goes on the application and it can lead to potential discrimination depending on how senior or junior you are.

o **Education.** This section is for formal education and should be no more than two lines per school. Just list the name of the school, city/state of the school, dates attended, expected completion date (month/year) of your degree, date you completed your degree, and major/minor as appropriate. Don't list units completed. That will go on the application and you don't have the room to spare on the resume. Additionally, if you have attended more than three educational institutions, just put the most appropriate two or three. They will all go on your application; you put what you want on the resume.

o **Shorten your margins, having them at 1 inch on all four sides will provide more space.** As needed, slightly decrease that number, adjust as needed.

- **Objective**. First of all, do have one at the top. Second, cater it to the department you're testing for (I hate generic resumes that look like you never change them). Personalize them to the department you're interviewing for, make us feel important and that we're you're number one (at least for now). Third, when you put the job title you are applying for on the resume, take it directly from the job flyer, and don't put what you think it is. *We were hiring for Firefighter/Engineer assigned to paramedic duty.* I saw titles such as:
  - o Firefighter/Paramedic
  - o Paramedic/Firefighter
  - o Firefighter/Engineer/Paramedic
  - o Firefighter/Engineer
  - o FF/P
  - o Firefighter/EMT-P
  - o Firefighter
  - o I know this may sound petty, but by not putting the exact job title on the application, it shows the department that you cannot follow written instructions and that you do not pay attention. These are both critical functions we expect of a firefighter. Additionally, by not putting the exact title, you run the risk of having your application discarded because of a department not currently testing for the position you applied for or not having a said position.
- **Don't assume that just because it is on your resume that we have seen and more importantly, will give you credit for it**. In an interview, remember the phrase "If you didn't say it, you didn't do it and don't get credit for it." If you're expecting us to give you credit for having something on the resume, what happens when the panel does not allow resumes? You're screwed. Treat every interview the same; make sure you cover everything (you feel are your key selling points) from your resume and application orally during the course of your interview.

- **Don't put your birth date on it.** Legally we cannot discriminate against you, don't give us any ammunition to load our gun with. Some departments like young candidates so they can mold them, some like older ones with more life experience and perceived maturity and some just don't care. My department doesn't even ask for your date of birth on the application. Yes, we can somewhat figure it out based on your high school graduation date, but don't put something on there that has the potential to work against you.
- **Spell check and grammar check.** What more do I need to say on this? Have someone that actually is very versed at the English language review it for you for errors and omissions.
- **Leave off the words "references available upon request."** We're not going to request them, we don't have time to look at them, and I bet many of you don't even bring them with you to offer if we did ask you for them. Rest assured, when it comes time for the background investigation, we'll ask you to write down the contact information for those references in the background investigation packet. Also, by offering them, you run the risk of having those names go against you. If you list people that are known by the board members as being not-so-stellar individuals (ones we wouldn't associate with), then you run the risk of having it go against you.
- **Names/addresses/phone numbers on the resume.** The only name on a resume should be your own. Not a place to put names of references or supervisors. The only address info should be your own; for employers, educational institutions, volunteer organizations, you should only put the city/state of that place (leave the street address off). The only phone number on the resume should be your own. Remember, all that information that I'm asking you to not put on there will go on the application. The resume is a shortened version of the application and you put on it what you want; versus we tell you what to put on the application.
- **Pronouns versus action verbs.** Keep the pronouns such as I off your resume. Instead, use action verbs to start off sentences. Looks more professional.

- **Pass it out at the beginning of the interview, not at the end.** At the end, we have typically come up with a preliminary overall score (won't be final until you are out of the room or the last candidate has completed their interview), and usually won't grade you on your resume alone, especially after the fact. Basically it will end up as something else to be filed or shredded to never see again. Having it at the beginning of the interview allows us to review it while you are talking and possibly even ask you questions off of it.

- **At least offer one.** I bet almost 50% of the candidates did not even offer us a resume. Don't assume that we have a copy of it. Our panel only had copies of your application to review.

- **Bring at least five copies.** One candidate passed out two resumes and asked if we could share them. Tacky, and unprofessional. If you don't have enough, don't even offer them.

- **Offer them to the panel; don't drop them in front of us.** Nobody likes anything forced down their throat, and some oral boards might not allow them at all. At least find a moment after being introduced to the panel to offer them. I found some candidates just dropping them in front of me while I started asking the first question, and I felt that to be rude.

- **Leaving it next to you to view during the interview.** The verdict is out on this one, and I'm not sure what I think. Numerous candidates actually passed out resumes to us, and then left one for themselves to view in front of them. On one hand, I think this is pretty ingenious so that you don't forget what to tell the board. On the other hand, I almost look at it as cheating. Just not sure what to make of this yet.

Job Applications:

- **Do spell check.** I saw a candidate misspell the name of his current fire department (that's bad) and almost one out of two applications had spelling errors.

- **If you can, type it out.** It looks more professional, especially since most people don't write neatly. Plus, having your wife write it out doesn't impress me either—we're trying to hire you, not your wife.
- **Fill in all the blanks.** I was amazed at how many candidates left blanks or even worse, put N/A in areas that were applicable. Some common areas where candidates did not complete the information required:
  - o Salary
  - o Reason for leaving your employer
  - o Supervisors name/contact information
  - o Dating the application after they signed it
  - o Education (yes, a couple of candidates put nothing in the box for all educational institutions attended).
  - o Job duties/Job title. Some candidates filled one out, but not the other.
- **Read all the questions.** Yes, there were some that only provided some of the information requested or provided information differing from what we requested.
- **Read everything carefully.**

General Things To NOT Tell The Oral Board:

- **Don't apologize for things; focus on the positive.** Some of the apologies I heard are:
  - o I'm probably the youngest one you'll see; please don't hold that against me. Why even say this?
  - o I don't have any education in fire science, but I'm willing to learn. I know that sounds sincere, but maybe just use the last half of the sentence (I'm willing to learn . . .).
  - o I really didn't have any time to research the department. Don't even bother.
  - o I'm not that experienced.
  - o I only had the chance to visit one fire station. Just say I visited a fire station and this is what I found out . . . .

o The list goes on; I would venture over half of the candidates apologized about something.

- **Don't state that you have learning disabilities or other major issues in life because it's going to make us look differently at you** (yes, I know legally we cannot, but it's hard not to). One person said he reads at the seventh grade level and is dyslexic. I'm just not convinced that is something you need to tell the oral boards. I think I know why he told us that, I'm assuming because he was trying to show an example of how he overcame something and is trying to get better. However, if you were an employer, do want that person trying to get better on your dime?

- **Don't mention your age.** Once again, we're not supposed to discriminate based on age. Don't give us more ammunition to sink you. Many candidates in their opening statement started out something to the effect of "my name is Steve and I am 39 years old, blah, blah, blah." Just don't go there.

- **Don't start crying, or getting teary eyed.** You might think that you're touching our sympathetic side, but we just don't find it professional. Many candidates had very tear-jerking stories to share with us. Yes, I felt sorry for them and sympathetic, but it didn't help their score in any way because I almost felt that they were trying to use that to have us gain sympathy for them (I was probably way off base, but it is what it is).

Our Fire Department:

- **At least know the name of the department.** One incorrectly called us by the wrong name eight separate times. For example, the candidate kept on saying "Santa Clara Fire" as opposed to "Santa Clara County Fire"—two different, but great fire departments. One time is understandable; eight times shows me you either don't care, you didn't do your research, or you just didn't properly prepare. If you can't get the name right now, how are you going to be when you're representing us in the public eye? We have enough problems as it is having people confuse us with Santa Clara <u>City</u> Fire Department. They are a great department, but they are not our department—two separate departments.

- **Name-dropping.** If you really feel compelled to name people in the department, at least ensure you are pronouncing them correctly. One candidate pronounced our fire chief's name wrong, and it is not that difficult of a name. My name, I understand; but even then, unless you can get it right, don't bother. Also on this subject, be careful of name-dropping. The names you think that might be stellar individuals might not be so stellar in the eye of the receiver. You might think that person helped you get the job, but in my eyes, I'm thinking otherwise because they incorrectly prepared you in some way.

- **Do better research.** Don't state facts that are incorrect (wrong number of stations, wrong number of apparatus—trucks, engines, etc.). One person said "you have a great budget." I don't know of any fire department that has a great budget. If it so great, why don't we have 4 person engine companies and more stations, newer apparatus, etc.? Don't get me wrong; we have an adequate budget, but nothing great. We don't transport patients; we provide ALS first responder services on our first out apparatus (engines, trucks, rescues and haz mat). Many candidates were answering questions like they were still a transport paramedic or that we were a transporting agency.

- **Be careful what you say.** Some examples "I know the streets really well." Yeah right, I bet if I gave you a street and told me to tell the board where it was located, which direction it ran, where it stopped and started, you probably wouldn't be able to. Don't open yourself up to failure. Plus, do you really know them that well? I doubt it. I bet you know the major streets, but we can teach anyone major streets.

- **Use appropriate terminology.** Many departments call their Truck Companies "Ladder Companies," their Ambulances

"Rescues," and so on. Not using proper terminology shows me you didn't do your research.

General Information:

- **Listening skills.** Most folks have terrible listening skills.
- **Time.** We only have so much time to give you—use it wisely. We told candidates you have 30 minutes for your interview. Usually the oral board only has 5 to 15 minutes to discuss and grade candidates, and go to the bathroom before the next candidate steps up for their 30 minutes in the hot seat. A few candidates felt it was their right to use up more than 30 minutes. I guess shame on us for not stopping them. We ended up running over, into our breaks, into our lunch hour, and into other candidate's times.
- **What to bring into the building besides yourself.** Resumes should be the only thing you bring into the building with you. Don't think you can leave your items on the chair outside the room either. One candidate brought in the daily paper (I assume he was reading it in the hallway while waiting his turn) and then put it on the interview table when he sat down. Just didn't work for me. **We don't want your certificates, references, letters of recommendations, or life stories contained within your binders.** We don't have time to look at that stuff—you're getting graded for what you say, not what is on paper. Plus, that stuff just takes up valuable table space.

Nervous Habits (That Distracted Us):

- **One candidate kicked the floor continuously.**
- **One candidate fidgeted with his ring so much it distracted me from what he was saying.**
- **Numerous candidates swiveled back and forth in the chair.**
- **The dreaded words—uhm, uh, ah, you know, etc.** These are all filler or slang words. Why do people say uhm or uh?

Because they are pausing, waiting to find something to say. One candidate had to have said uhm over 100 times. Instead of saying uhm or uh, pause and remain silent. Force yourself to be aware of your speech and you will improve. Yes, you are getting graded on oral communications and we want to have people that will represent us very well, every time you are giving station tours, public education demonstrations, talking to the media, or just talking to the general public in your everyday work. Here are my suggestions to improve your speech:

- o **Be aware of what you are saying at all times, have your "edit feature" working.** Awareness is half the battle; doing something about it is the other half.
- o **Listen to yourself answer questions in a tape recorder or through a video camera during mock orals.** Yes, that is you you're listening to, as painful as it may sound (I know, I hate listening to myself on tape).
- o **Take some speech classes at a college.**
- o **Take every opportunity to stand up in front of audiences and speak or teach classes.**
- o **Join Toastmasters.** You'll not only improve your oral communications, but your leadership skills as well.
- o **Watch the news reporters deliver their news stories.** Most newscasters are excellent oral communicators; they have to be or they would be out of a job. Nobody wants to watch the news just to be put to sleep. Newscasters punch their words, accentuate and emphasize their words, modulate their speech as needed, and do not sound as monotone or boring as most candidates do during an oral interview.
- o **Don't learn from athletes or musicians.** Athletes are not getting paid for their speaking ability; they are getting paid for their athletic ability. That said, just because a famous ball player is saying "you know" and

"like" or other slang words consistently, it doesn't mean you have to follow their lead.

Political Correctness:

- **Agree with it or not, but you have to try to be politically correct.** If nothing else to show the board you have an edit feature and you can represent us well in the public eye.
- **I heard fireman a few times.** If you have a female grading you, this could be the kiss of death; even if there is not a female on the oral board, it could show the males that you are unprofessional, immature, inappropriate or just plain clueless.
- **Old people should probably not be called old people; instead try "elderly."**
- **Be nice to everyone you come in contact with in life, but especially when you are in the testing process.** You never know who you will be talking to and if I was a fire chief making hiring decisions, I would be asking all of my staff, including secretaries, to provide their feedback as to how nice you were and how you treated them. When it is 3 a.m. and the fire chief is at home sleeping, he or she wants to know you'll be representing the department in the best light when nobody else is watching.

Attire:

- **Take a look in the mirror.** I saw candidates that had a gap between their shirt top button and their tie. Tighten it up, and straighten that tie.
- **Shave the stuff under your chin (and under your lip), you're not trying to score a date or look cool.** You're trying to get a job. Don't wait for us to offer the job before you shave the stuff we may not let you have on your face on the job. You may never get the job offer as we don't want to have to change you, we want you to change for us.

- **Dress shoes.** Please polish them before you show up to the interview.
- **Dry-clean the suit.** I saw some candidates that looked like they had slept in their suit because of all of the wrinkles.

Education:

- **If you're going to start something—finish it.** This includes education. So many candidates have not finished their formal education. The ones that did get degrees really stuck out; getting the degree doesn't guarantee you the job, but it makes you stand out positively and prove to the board that you can finish something and you have a basic level of education to offer.
- **If you don't have any fire education on your resume, do what it takes to get some!** Go to your local junior college and start working towards that two year degree in fire technology and get into a firefighter academy as well. Take as many fire classes as you can to show your commitment to the fire service. There were many paramedics that had years of experience on a private ambulance, but did not have a clue about what the job of a firefighter entails or what the fire service does and stands for. Just because you work on an ambulance and respond to calls with the firefighters doesn't mean that you have a clue as to what we do or why we do what we do. Getting some college fire technology education will be one way to make you have a more, well rounded background. Just because you have a lot of paramedic or EMT experience on an ambulance, it doesn't mean that you're going to be a sure thing for the department. We're not hiring licenses or experience. We're hiring people that we hope will turn out to be successful assets to the department and the community for many years.

Oral Interview Opening Statement Related:

- **Do have it written out and prepared in advance.** There is a great chance at every interview (no guarantee) that you will have the opportunity to provide an opening statement. Something to the effect of "tell us how you have prepared yourself," "tell the board how your education, experience and background have prepared you for a position with our department," etc. These questions, like the closing statement, are the freebies. There is no reason you shouldn't nail this one, assuming you have prepared and practiced in advance.

- **What I suggest is having it on your computer so you can modify it as needed.** Yes, it should be continuously changing as you add more information to it and you find things that need to be added, deleted, or altered.

- **Keep it under five minutes, preferably under four minutes.**

- **Contain the information found in your resume and application, as well as some personal characteristics.** Don't assume we'll give you credit for something on the resume or application; if you don't say it, you don't get credit for it. Talk about your training, education (formal), experience, community service, bilingual ability, personal characteristics and attributes.

- **Don't tell us your age or name in the opening statement.** For that matter, sorry to sound harsh, but I really don't care to hear about the names of each of your five children, three dogs and two cats. I'd love to find out their names if we hire you as I get to know you better, but for the purposes of the interview, I don't think it's appropriate. You can say you're married with kids, but then move on.

Oral Interview Closing Statement Related:

- **Keep it from 30 seconds to 90 seconds, nothing more, and nothing less.** When we asked them do you have anything else to say, we heard everything from "thank you very much, I appreciate the chance to be here" to five minute dissertations. Anything over 90 seconds is going to bore us and possibly hurt your score, especially if it makes you go over your allotted time.

- **Show us your passion for wanting to be here with us, in our department.** Some candidates did not do this, and it sounded like they just wanted any fire job. At least make us feel like we are your number one choice, and hopefully in a sincere way.

Answering Oral Board Questions:

- **Don't ask us at the end of every answer you provide, "does that answer the question," or "is that specific enough?"** Our standard answer was "whatever you feel is appropriate."
- **Don't abruptly end your answers.** It makes us wonder if you have anything more to say. Have a nice closing to each question, even if it is only one sentence.
- **Don't immediately blurt out your answer.** It makes it seem like you heard the questions in advance. On that note, don't share the questions with your buddies; you're only hurting yourself.
- **Take a few seconds to process the question and formulate an answer.** However, don't take that too literally and spend up to two minutes (or so it seemed) trying to find an answer. There were a few candidates I almost wanted to do a pulse check on or shake and shout to ensure they were still alive. Annie, Annie, are you ok??? Sorry, old school CPR reference.
- **Don't ramble on, get to your point, but be detailed.** Saying something without backing it up is not going to get you hired. For example, don't say "I am dependable." Back it up with a fact/ example and maybe why it is important to be dependable. That will take your score from an average 70% score on that question to a score in the 80 to 90 percentile. 70% answers don't get you the job; 80% and 90% answers do.
- **Before you answer, don't tell the board "this is a tough question," or "this is not what I expected," or "that is a good question."** Do you think we would ask you easy questions?

That just doesn't make you look to confident or prepared. You should expect any and all types of questions. If you have answers for virtually every type of question we can ask you, you'll be able to adapt to answer anything asked of you.

Info Specific To The Position You're Applying For:

- **If you are applying for a paramedic position, expect to have questions to test your knowledge, skills and abilities you are claiming to possess.**
  - o   May be actual hands-on skills scenarios
  - o   May be oral questions
- **While you are not expected to know our specific county EMS protocols to do well, it wouldn't hurt to know them.** Most county EMS agencies have websites with their protocols (policies and procedures) online to download. Knowing county protocols in advance is a "value-added" answer. On that note, it doesn't hurt to know your ACLS or PALS protocols as well. Then, when describing your treatment, it doesn't hurt you to say "in Santa Clara County, I know the protocol is _____," or "where I work in San Francisco, our protocol is_____."
- **Some fire departments actually have their paramedic candidates perform a hands-on skills examination.** A common one is to have you come into a room and run an adult or pediatric full arrest, or demonstrate your knowledge of treating different patients or reading different cardiac rhythms. Other items you should expect to be tested on include seldom-used skills. Discussions I have had with fire departments that use such skills assessment centers within their paramedic testing process tell me that it is not uncommon to have 50% or more of the candidates fail this station, thus removing them from the hiring process.
- **We actually had a paramedic scenario that was more of a talking station where you talked your way through your patient treatment.** I figured it would be easier and was

expecting more candidates to pass. Well, our results were not much different from other fire departments out there. You might be great at what you do in the field, but if you can't talk your way through the station, you're not going to succeed.

- **Some of the main reasons candidates did not do well in the paramedic scenario:**
    - o Too aggressive in their treatment
    - o Not aggressive enough in their treatment
    - o Not having a clue as to what to do
    - o Totally missing the primary chief complaint and deviating into other treatments that would not have benefited the patient as much as the treatments we were looking for.
    - o Incorrect dosages, incorrect routes of administration, incorrect concentrations or names of medications to be used
    - o Reading too much into the scenario
    - o Not checking for expiration dates
    - o Lack of confidence in their treatment plan (saying "I would consider" or "I think I would do this."). We want confident, not cocky, paramedics to represent us.
    - o Not being detailed enough; remember, if you didn't say it, you didn't do it!
    - o Not having a good detailed patient turnover report (most were pathetic at best).
    - o Not reviewing the equipment we put in front of you. If we take the time to put some equipment in front of you, if you're given the chance to review it, please touch and handle everything and ask any questions immediately if you are not familiar with something. Also, if there are medications check the expiration dates and ask questions if something is expired. There were expired and current medications and only a few people noticed the difference.

Just some random thoughts, hope they help in some form or fashion. Realize that these are just my opinions and that opinions can and do change from person to person and department to department. What may be considered inappropriate to say or do in one department may be different in another. For example, some departments still use the term fireman in some capacity, while most do not. Learn something from every person you come in contact with, both from the good and the not so good. Good luck, there is an oral interview out there in your future if you don't give up!

# # # #

CHAPTER 7

The Chief's Interview

Usually one of the last phases of the hiring process is the Chief's Interview. By the time you reach the Chief's interview, you have had an initial oral interview with a panel of individuals that could be from the ranks of Firefighter up through Deputy Chief. From there, many fire departments then take the highest-ranking candidates on further through the process (background investigations, medical examinations, psychological evaluations, etc.).

Going through a Chief's Interview usually means that you are one of the candidates that are being considered for a position. Not every fire department requires candidates to also go through a Chief's Interview. If you do get invited to a Chief's Interview it could be with any of the following individuals: just the Fire Chief, the Fire Chief and a member or members of his/her executive staff (other ranking chief officers such as Assistant Chiefs, Deputy Chiefs, Division Chiefs, or Battalion Chiefs), or a few of the ranking chief officers without the Fire Chief. Every department is different.

Either way, the Chief's Interview is set up to find out more about you on a personal basis (versus the initial oral interview which is really used as an initial screening process to determine which candidates at least meet the minimum requirements to work for the department). While a Chief's Interview is a little less formal than the initial oral interview, it is still very critical that you make a positive, lasting impression with the individuals interviewing you. This is where the "buck usually stops" and they are determining whether or not you will fit the culture of their department.

Not everyone that successfully passes the first oral interview will receive an invitation to the chief's interview. Most departments employ the "rule of 3," the rule of 5," "the rule of 10," or "the rule of the list." What this means is:

- **Rule of 3:** If there are five vacancies to hire for, the chief can interview the top 15 candidates on the hiring list (three people interviewed for each open position for a total of 15 people interviewed for the five open positions).
- **Rule of 5:** If there are five vacancies to hire for, the chief can interview the top 25 candidates on the hiring list (25 people interviewed for the five open positions).
- **Rule of 10:** If there are five vacancies to hire for, the chief can interview the top 50 candidates on the hiring list (50 people interviewed for the five open positions.
- **Rule of the list:** If there are five vacancies to hire for, the chief can interview ANYONE on the hiring list, regardless of final ranking or position on the list.

Depending on the civil service rules established by the department, the city, the county or whoever has the ultimate authority for hiring personnel, any of the above formulas may be employed. Based on the above formulas, you can see that just because you are number one on a hiring list, it doesn't guarantee you a job or position in the upcoming recruit academy. You still have to earn your spot. Many people think that the above rules are unfair and that the fire chief should hire candidates straight from the top of the list down. Meaning if there are five positions to hire for, numbers one through five should get the first five job offers.

While that seems to be fair to those top five candidates, realize why departments employ various rules:

- It allows them options and choices.

- Just because you are number one, it does not mean you are the best candidate. I'll argue my point because some people are good test takers (don't get me wrong, you have to be a good test-taker to get hired or succeed in the fire service) and the difference between the top ten (or top hundred) candidates could be very, very small in the way of percentage points. If number one has an overall score of 95.3%, number ten has an overall score of 94.9%, and number 55 has an overall score of 94.1% after all the phases of the hiring process have been graded, can you really tell me that with a 1.2% difference between 55 candidates, that number one will actually make that much better of a firefighter than number 55 will? I doubt it. Realize to get that final ranking, the score is typically either based 100% on the oral interview or as a combination of the oral interview and the written examination. The oral interview can be very subjective and does not really tell us how successful a person will be as a firefighter. It is a screening tool that does the best it can.
- Plus, let's say number one was determined to be the best candidate by the oral board. However, upon closer examination, it is determined that the number one candidate has had been arrested numerous times for various offences (driving under the influence, assaulting a police officer, possession of narcotics, etc.). How did that person come out number one with a record like that? Because many oral boards do not have access to a person's application (which would have included information such as arrest records) and most oral boards don't ask if you have ever been arrested. So, in theory it is very possible to have a candidate smoke the interview questions but have a less than desirable background. The candidate is number one, but would you really want to take a chance on someone with such a less than stellar track record? I wouldn't want that potential liability. If the fire chief did not have a requirement to use a rule of three (or whatever rule) when interviewing candidates, and just hired firefighters straight down the list, then a person like this could squeeze through the cracks. Does it mean they would not make

a great firefighter? Of course not. However, as they say, the best predictor of future behavior is past behavior. Multiple arrests does not show responsibility or maturity, among other things. Oh wait, now they are reformed and are sorry for their mistakes. So would I if I wanted to be a firefighter now.

- It allows them to ensure that diversity candidates have a chance to be hired.
- It allows them to hire people based on qualifications (for example, number five might be bilingual in English and Spanish, whereas the first four candidates are not).

A chief's interview will typically last 20 minutes to 60 minutes, and will usually be more in depth than the first oral interview. The chief will probably have had more than ample time to read your resume, read your application, and review any notes from the first oral board.

Be prepared for such questions as:

- Tell me how you've prepared yourself for the position?
- Tell me about yourself?
- Why do you want to work for our department?
- What do you know about our department?
- What do you know about our community?
- Where do you see yourself in five years? Ten years? Fifteen years?
- What is your career development plans?
- Clarifications or explanations for items on your resume or application.
- Why should I hire you over all of the other candidates?
- If I hire you, are you going to leave our department for another department if you get a better offer or find a department that is closer to your home?
- Where do you think the fire service is headed as industry?
- What are the biggest issues facing the fire service today?
- What does customer service mean to you?
- Can you give us an example of outstanding customer service you have provided?

- What does it mean to be a professional firefighter?
- Tell me what you know about our Department Strategic Plan? (Or any other key document available on the Department website or made available to the public).
- Tell me a time when you were emotionally charged and how did you handle yourself?

The chief's interview can be very intimidating, but it should not be. Don't get me wrong, it is not going to be laid back and casual, and you probably will not get the red carpet treatment, but it shouldn't have to be so stressful on you that you vapor lock and pass out. Realize the fire chief and their chief officers are human beings, just like you. Whether the fire chief is wearing a suit or their class A uniform with all of the gold accessories blinding your eyes, your delivery and actions should be the same. Treat it like you would any other interview, and do not let your guard down.

Some tips to help you prepare for the Chief's interview:

- Do some research on the Fire Chief (name, picture, background—educational, experience, personal) to ensure you have a good idea of who is interviewing you. The Internet can assist here, as can current fire service personnel working for the Department (fire station visits). Remember people tend to like those that are like them, so the more commonalities you may possess, the better your chances may be!
- Know as much as you can about the Department (vision, values, mission statement, core values, strategic plan, business plan, etc.).
- Know yourself inside and outside. Seriously. Know what you have to offer the Department now and 30 years from now. Know what positions/ranks you aspire to. Know your career development and personal development goals. Know your training and education goals. Know how you plan to leave that Department and the fire service in general better than you found it.

- Relax, be yourself—answer questions the way you feel you would answer them, NOT how you think they want you to answer them.
- Review your initial application, as well as your resume and anything you have submitted to the Department; you may get asked questions about anything from your background.
- Be prepared for ANY type of question you may be asked. There are no trick questions if you've properly prepared. Have examples from every class you've attended, every job you've ever held, and anything else you've been involved with to be able to tie into questions you're asked.
- Remember a Fire Chief is looking for someone who is and has a track record of being mature, responsible, ethical, empathetic, compassionate, accountable, motivated, loyal, a hard worker, dedicated, dependable, and gets what it means to be a firefighter. Be able to show you have the necessary characteristics to join their team.
- Smart Fire Chiefs are interviewing entry-level candidates and looking for future Captains, future Battalion Chiefs, future Deputy Chiefs and even their future replacement. I'm not saying to walk in and say you're going to be Fire Chief in 10 years because that's probably unrealistic. I'm saying to not downplay your career development goals and to be able to be confident, yet not cocky about where you want to be in your career.

# # # #

CHAPTER 8

The Background Investigation

Prior to the job offer, the last component of the typical hiring process in most fire departments is the background investigation. Private companies that employ trained investigators typically complete most background investigations. Some fire departments may also use their local law enforcement personnel with specialized training in the area of investigations, and a few may even attempt to do their own, which is probably not recommendable unless their personnel have the necessary knowledge, skills and abilities to do a great job. If you have never completed a public safety background investigation packet, you're in for a surprise!

Most background investigation packets are about 20 to 40 pages in length. They're basically a job application on steroids. Whereas most job applications are typically 3 to 7 pages long and basically scratch the surface in regards to your background, the background investigation packet goes into full detail on every aspect of your life including but not limited to:

- Personal information
- Relatives, friends, and references
- Residence information
- Work experience
- Life experience
- Disciplinary history

- Military experience
- Educational history
- Financial history
- Legal history
- Law enforcement activity
- Driving record (accidents, tickets, proof of insurance)
- Drug / medication usage

If you have never completed a background packet, I encourage you to do so PRIOR to getting asked to do so by a public safety agency. Why? Because if you attempt to gather all of this information on the first try, it will be very overwhelming and somewhat stressful. Seriously.

Nobody is perfect, myself included. The key for you as a candidate to ensure you are as successful as you can be during a background investigation is to be honest, be complete, and be accurate. In short, have a high attention to detail. Background investigators are trained to look for inconsistencies and inaccuracies, as well as patterns of both. It's not necessarily what you've done (bad stuff) as much as how well you document what you've done, and how well you take responsibility and accountability for your actions and non-actions. Time does heal things, and as long as you have not made the same mistake twice you should be ok (unless it was something really bad like a felony). Realize what one department considers ok or bad may not be the same in the next department. Each department has it's own criteria for what they will accept and not accept in a candidate.

How to prepare for your background investigation:

1. The best thing to do is complete a blank background packet in advance.

   a. For a sample background investigation packet to download and complete (strongly encouraged), visit my websites:
      - http://www.chabotfire.com (firefighter hiring process components link) <u>or</u>

- http://www.code3firetraining.com
  (free stuff link)
- If you cannot locate it, email me at sprziborowski
  @aol.com and I will send you one.
- I realize this will probably take you weeks to complete; that's ok. It's better to take the time now as opposed to when you're under the gun trying to locate all the information.
- While this may not be the same background packet required of the department who puts you through a background, the information asked for is typically the same.

2. Create a binder with that completed background packet in it that contains answers to the following questions, as well as the additional documentation and/or information that you will typically be asked to provide to support the questions below:

   a. Complete educational transcripts (unofficial versus official)
      - Dates attended, units earned, addresses, etc.
      - Copies of any diplomas received
   b. Copies of all of your certificates you claim to have received (you may be also asked to provide the original copy)
   c. Selective Service documentation (are you registered for the draft? If not, get on it)
   d. Military documentation (discharge paperwork, time spent, addresses, etc.)
   e. Medical records / immunization records (current TB, MMR, vaccinations, Hepatitis B, etc.)
   f. Alcohol / drug usage history
   g. Motor vehicle operation history
      - Accidents (dates, circumstances, injuries, etc.)
      - Traffic and parking tickets (dates, circumstances, fees paid, etc.)

- Insurance information (company, agent, policy numbers, etc.)
- Vehicle owned (year, make, model, color, license #, etc.)

h. Legal related
- Arrest record
- All convictions
- Lawsuits you have been involved in
- Groups you have been involved with that advocate violence dissent or overthrow of the U.S. Government
- Participation in the illegal use of any explosives or fire bombs
- Participation as a member of an extremist group or organization

i. Employment information
- Names, addresses, phone numbers of all of your employers and supervisors
- Can be expected to go back ten years or more
- Work discipline records
- Work attendance and tardiness records
- Your past job titles, duties, and salaries

j. Personal information
- Names, addresses, phone numbers of family members, friends, relatives, and acquaintances
- Listing of all you past residences
- Copy of your birth certificate
- Copy of your driver's license

k. Financial and credit history.
- Have you ever been bonded? Ever have a bond refused?
- Ever been delinquent on any court ordered payment?
- Ever failed to support any child born to you?
- Ever had your wages attached or garnished?

- Ever filed for or declared bankruptcy?
- If you haven't done so already, get your free credit reports from the 3 major companies (which you can do once a year free):
  - o Experian: http://www.experian.com
  - o Equifax: http://www.equifax.com
  - o Transunion: http://www.transunion.com

Key Point: Since this is all very confidential information, do what it takes to keep the information safe and secure.

Items that may eliminate you from the hiring process (can vary from agency to agency):

- Current use of any illegal drug, including prescription drugs not prescribed to applicant.
- Any illegal drug use within the past 2 years.
- Convicted of any Domestic Violence offense.
- Felony conviction to include felony traffic offenses.
- Conviction for Driving Under the Influence of Alcohol (DUI), Driving Under the Influence of Drugs (DUID), or Driving While Ability Impaired (DWAI) within the last 3 years.
- Dishonorable or Bad Conduct Discharge from the United States Armed Forces.
- Theft, dishonesty, and any other character issues that may bring discredit to you and/or your employment with the F.D., in the event you were given an offer of employment.
- Suicide attempts.
- Use of any hallucinogenic drug (LSD, PCP, acid, angel dust, mushrooms).
- More than one DUI conviction.
- No high school diploma or G.E.D.
- Being on probation or parole.
- Lack of U.S. citizenship or eligibility.

- Any sex acts in which you were an adult and the other party/parties were under the age of 18 years old.
- Any sex acts perpetrated against the will of the other party.
- Any drug-related conviction, including a disposition involving diversion.
- Any adult conviction for a theft related offense within the past five years, including conviction that was disposed of through diversion.
- Use of any injected steroid.
- Military discipline: court martial/General or dishonorable discharge.
- Failing to submit all required documentation in a complete, neat, and timely fashion.
- Failing to keep scheduled appointments.
- Any false statement or any intentional omission of information, either on the employment application, the personal history statement, the pre-investigative questionnaire, or verbally to the oral board or background investigator.
- More than three moving violations within the last three years.
- A history of driver's license suspensions or revocations; lack of automobile insurance.
- Any failures to appear on driving records.
- Being at fault in three or more traffic collisions within the past three years.

I have heard of fire departments that have given candidates only a week to return the completed background packet. If you have never completed a background packet and need to obtain all of the information required for the first time, you're going to be in a world of hurt. Take the time to gather as much as the information now so that you're prepared when you're asked to complete the background investigation packet.

Once you submit the background investigation packet, the next step may be to meet with someone from the fire department and/or the background investigator to clarify or confirm the information within. If you're successful at the background investigation, the next step of the hiring process in many departments is to receive a conditional job offer and then be sent to a medical (fit for duty) examination with the department's physician, and maybe even a psychological examination and/or a polygraph (lie detector test) examination to be able to provide the department with as much background as they can on the person they are debating about making a very important decision on hiring.

To quote Dennis Rubin, retired Fire Chief of the District of Columbia Fire Department (DCFD): "Don't hire thugs, misfits or idiots!"

Unfortunately many fire departments fail to receive that Memo and end up hiring thugs, misfits and/or idiots—and pay the price for many years to come. The sad part is that many fire departments do not do an adequate job at the background investigation process, or look the other way when presented with candidates with questionable backgrounds for a variety of reasons. Then when the person turns out to be the bad apple, they seem surprised that the person was not a good fit for the fire service. Pay now or pay later . . .

# # # #

CHAPTER 9

The Medical Examination

One of the last phases of the firefighter hiring process is the medical examination, where the candidate is sent to a physician that is chosen by the fire department to evaluate candidates, and to determine if they are fit for duty, and have the necessary capacity to serve as a firefighter. Firefighting is not for everyone. Years ago, if someone had a "bad back" or "bad knees," they would probably be failed out of the process. But today, thanks to the numerous laws protecting employees (not protecting employers), such as the Americans' with Disabilities Act, those that may have been disqualified for such conditions in the past stand a great chance at getting hired today.

In most departments, the medical examination is offered AFTER the candidate receives a conditional job offer. Meaning if you fail a part of the medical examination, you have the ability to find a second opinion to prove you can do the job. With the amount of lawyers and doctors in the world, if you want this job bad enough, you can get a second opinion in your favor.

The department-designated physician will usually evaluate you based on the criteria determined by the National Fire Protection Association (NFPA) Standard 1582 (Standard on Occupational Medical Program for Fire Departments). Internet research can provide you with more information on NFPA 1582, something you should do ASAP to ensure you're not wasting a lot of valuable time trying to obtain a career you may not be qualified for. But, don't just give up if you see something that may disqualify you. Take the time to get a second and third opinion from qualified individuals from different departments, including the departments you are applying for. Qualified individuals include the department human resources or personnel services division. I would caution you from relying on the advice from personnel working at the fire stations only because they are probably not up-to-date with all of the current medical requirements as someone from human resources would be. Nothing personal, it is what it is.

NFPA 1582 is the road map for department physicians to ensure those candidates that want to be firefighters are actually fit and capable of performing the necessary functions of the position.

The physician will do a complete physical to evaluate your past medical history as well as your current condition, including but not limited to the following areas:

- Weight
- Vision
- Hearing
- Blood Pressure
- Heart
- Lungs
- Skin
- Gastrointestinal
- Limbs
- Musculoskeletal/Skeletal
- Neurological
- Surgical history
- Hospitalization history
- Health conditions
- Social activities that may include alcohol use, smoking, exercise, diet, and stress

You are encouraged to learn as much as you can about NFPA 1582 and how it may apply to you and your situation. The bottom line is that each fire department is slightly different than the next. What one may disqualify a candidate for may differ from the next.

# # # #

CHAPTER 10

The Psychological Examination

Before, after or during the time a candidate is scheduled for the medical examination, they may also be sent to a licensed psychologist for a psychological evaluation. If you thought filling out a background investigation packet was fun—wait until you have to sit down and take a test that can consist of upwards of 1,000 questions over the course of a half-day or full-day! It actually isn't 1,000 different questions as much as it is about 100 or less questions asked 10 or more different ways, to look for consistency or inconsistency in your answers.

The first part of the psychological examination is usually that written test, followed on the same day or a different day by a review with a psychologist to ask you follow-up questions based on your answers. Remember that the psychologist is not your friend! That doesn't mean be dishonest (you better be as honest as you can), it means be careful about being deceived to answer questions a certain way. As they say, "anything you say, can be held or used against you . . . ." But, don't think that's a license to shut your mouth and say nothing. That can be worse than spilling the beans and admitting to things you've never even done just because you feel under the gun or under pressure to demonstrate your honesty.

I remember the psychologist having reviewed the answers to the thousand or so questions, and then in the process of asking certain questions, asking me the question, "when was the last time you were angry?" I honestly couldn't think of a moment. I paused, and I looked at her and said, "I honestly don't remember." She continued to stare at me waiting for me to say something. Under the pressure, I stupidly mumbled something to the effect of "sitting here, having to answer such questions." Thinking she had a sense of humor was mistake number 1. Thinking I was great at making people laugh was mistake number 2. Oh, talk about the deafening silence and death stare that subsequently occurred . . . Realizing I may have just shot myself in the foot, I tried to backtrack and apologize for the inappropriate comment and for not taking the process seriously and professionally. In the end it worked out, but I learned a valuable lesson that could have been a negative outcome—don't try to make the psychologist laugh. Answer the questions, be honest, do the best you can, don't make up things, be mature and be professional.

The psychologist may or may not have had a chance to see your background investigation packet. Regardless, the questions you are asked during the psychological examination are very similar to the background investigation—just asked in many different formats. The reason they are the same is so the department can look for consistencies or inconsistencies, as well as patterns of good or bad behavior in their pursuit of determining if you will be a good fit for their department.

After the psychologist has met with you, they will usually package their results of your examination and interview to the fire department for final review and approval. It is not uncommon for some psychologists to rate candidates with a school grade schedule: A, B, C, D and F. If a candidate is an A or B, the department can be pretty confident the candidate will be a good fit and not have any significant issues. If a candidate is a C, then the department really needs to evaluate why the candidate received such a score before they say yes or no. If a candidate is a D or an F, then the department can still choose to hire the person, but would be foolish to do so (buyer beware as they say) given the information that was obtained during the psychological evaluation.

While the psychological examination process is not perfect (no part of the hiring process is perfect), it is a necessary tool for a department to use, in addition to the other components of the hiring process (written test, oral interview, background investigation, chief's interview, etc.) at determining who may be a good fit for a department.

It is not uncommon to have a handful of candidates wash out (get eliminated) of the hiring process because of the psychological examination for a variety of reasons—each of which may differ from department to department and Fire Chief to Fire Chief. While some firefighters believe the psychological examination is useless, it is a valuable tool in my experience, because it allows you into a part of a person most of us never are allowed to see or experience. I have known firefighters on the job to complain that so-and-so should have been hired, even though they may have failed or not done well in the psychological examination, because "I know them and they're a great guy or gal."

Well, my experience will allow me to respectfully disagree with that uneducated statement. We may think we know others, even close friends and/or family members, but at the end of the day—how well do we really know them? I don't mean to sound negative, but how many times have you seen someone get arrested for say a mass murder and the family or neighbors or friends of the suspect are saying something to the effect of "he's innocent," or "he could not have done that," or "that is so unlike him," or something similar—only to then have a jury of 12 convict him for the crime he "supposedly could never do because he was such a nice person or a great friend or whatever." Too many times, more than I care to mention. That's why when firefighters try to put in a plug for someone they know in the process, I of course listen, but I also try to tell them that that the person is at the mercy of the overall process and that if they fail out of the process, it may be for reasons you are not privy too. Don't get me wrong, some of our best firefighters were referred to us by other firefighters or have come through our volunteer firefighter program. But, we have also hired many great firefighters who lived out-of-state and we met the first time they started visiting stations to prepare for their oral interview. We never know; smart fire departments keep an open mind, don't get emotionally attached to candidates, and evaluate all of the necessary information on a specific candidate.

We realize nobody is perfect. Everyone has probably done something they regret or are ashamed of. Your key is to be honest, be consistent, and take responsibility and accountability for your actions or non-actions.

# # # #

CHAPTER 11

The Recruit Academy

When a fire department hires you as a firefighter, they will usually put you through a recruit academy lasting anywhere from one week to six months in duration. These academies usually run from 8:00 a.m. to 5:00 p.m. (or some other variation lasting from 8 hours to 10 hours per day) and last the entire week, from Monday through Friday. The typical length of a recruit academy is 8 weeks to 24 weeks. Even if you have already completed a firefighter academy at a community college or through another fire department where you had previously worked as a firefighter, you will still usually have to go through a full academy (unless the department requires a firefighter 1 certificate and/or firefighter 1 academy completion certificate—if they do, then sometimes they only have a one or two week mini-academy to orient you to the way they do things).

Why would I still want to complete a firefighter 1 academy through a community college if the fire department is going to put me through one anyway? Well, first of all, having completed a firefighter 1 academy at a community college allows you to apply for more firefighter tests since some departments require you to have completed an academy just to take their test. Second, it is not uncommon for newly hired firefighters to be terminated (fired) during their recruit academy for various reasons such as poor physical conditioning, attitude problems, discipline problems, tardiness problems, substandard scores on their written tests and / or skills tests, etc.

Getting terminated by one fire department is not the end of the world, but it definitely does not increase your chances of getting hired by another fire department in the future. Going through a firefighter 1 academy offered at a community college first lets you know your strengths and weaknesses and proves to you (and others including fire departments) that you should have what it takes to get hired as a firefighter and keep your job as a firefighter.

Some of the community college firefighter 1 academies have reputations of being more challenging and demanding than some academies that are put on by fire departments for their new recruits. Successfully completing one of these academies not only looks good on your resume, but also helps set you up for success when you finally get hired by your dream fire department.

I was sure happy that I had gone through Chabot's firefighter 1 academy prior to going through the recruit academy when I was hired as a full-time firefighter. Many of my recruit academy classmates had NEVER been through an academy before (or had even taken any fire technology classes), and it really made it difficult for some of them because they were learning information for the first time and having to really study hard and for long hours in the evenings and weekends when the academy wasn't occurring. Since I had already been through an academy before (which had used the same textbook), going through my department's recruit academy was not that stressful because I was just reviewing and refreshing what I had already learned.

Many fire department recruit academies require you to maintain an 80% average on ALL written test scores. Not maintaining an 80% average can (and sometimes does) lead to termination! Are you doing this now in your fire technology classes? If not, then you better find out what it takes to increase your scores so this does not happen to you.

The most common textbooks that are utilized in recruit academies that I am aware of are:

- <u>Essentials of Firefighting</u>, published by the International Fire Service Training Association (IFSTA).
- <u>Firefighter's Handbook</u>, published by Delmar Publishers.

- <u>Fundamentals of Firefighter Skills</u>, published by Jones & Bartlett Publishers.

It is my experience that most fire technology degree programs and academies utilize one of the above textbooks (at Chabot, we utilize the <u>Essentials of Firefighting</u> by IFSTA).

The typical day at a recruit academy may start off with physical conditioning/physical fitness, have you complete a multiple-choice written test, and then combine the rest of the day with lectures on various firefighting topics such as:

- Fire behavior
- Fire investigation
- Fire prevention
- Utilization of ladders and hose
- Cultural diversity
- History of the fire service and of the department you are working for
- Manipulative (hands-on) skills practice and testing on performing various firefighting practices such as:
  - Ladder evolutions
  - Hose evolutions (structure and wildland)
  - Individual performance standards (donning an SCBA, pulling a pre-connected hose-line, etc.)
  - Team performance standards (simulated fire attack evolutions, rescue procedures, etc.)
  - Rescue practices

# # # #

Sample Recruit Academy Schedule

Week 1:

Monday:
AM—Orientation, Rules & Regulations; PPE & Safety Clothing.
PM—SCBA

Tuesday:
AM—Sexual Harassment & Diversity Training
PM—Fire Service Organization; Fitness Lecture/Testing

Wednesday:
AM—PPE/SCBA Drill; Academy Logistics
PM—EMS Introduction; Axe Maintenance & Techniques

Thursday:
AM & PM—Ladders Part 1, Fitness & Conditioning

Friday:
AM—Weekly Individual Performance Testing (IPT)—SCBA, 16' Ladder, Axe use
PM—Recruit Counseling, Skills Practice, EMS Skills, Fitness & Conditioning.

Week 2:

Monday:
AM & PM—Hose Part 1

Tuesday:
AM & PM—Ladders Part 2

Wednesday:
AM—Apparatus Familiarization
PM—EMS Introduction

Thursday:
AM & PM—Ropes, Knots & Slings, Tools Aloft, Fitness & Conditioning

Friday:
AM—Weekly Individual Performance Testing (IPT)—SCBA, Forward Lay, 16' Ladder, Tools Aloft, Axe use
PM—Recruit Counseling, Skills Practice, EMS Skills, Fitness & Conditioning.

Week 3:

Monday:
AM & PM—Search & Rescue, Fitness & Conditioning

Tuesday:
AM & PM—Specialized Tools, Fitness & Conditioning

Wednesday:
AM & PM—Hose Part 2

Thursday:
AM & PM—Ladders Part 3, Fitness & Conditioning

Friday:
AM—Weekly Individual Performance Testing (IPT)—SCBA, Pre-Connect Hose Line, Search Operations, Roof Ladder Aloft, Axe use.
PM—Recruit Counseling, Skills Practice, EMS Skills, Fitness & Conditioning.

Week 4:

Monday:
AM & PM—State Certified Low Angle Rope Rescue Operational

Tuesday:
AM & PM—State Certified Low Angle Rope Rescue Operational

Wednesday:
AM & PM—State Certified Low Angle Rope Rescue Operational, Fitness & Conditioning

Thursday:
AM & PM—Fire Behavior

Friday:
AM—Weekly Individual Performance Testing (IPT)—Pre-Connect Hose Line, Search Operations, Roof Ladder Aloft, Z-Rig, Axe use. PM—Recruit Counseling, Skills Practice, EMS Skills, Fitness & Conditioning, AWR-160 On Line Class.

Week 5:

Monday:
AM & PM—State Certified Firefighter Survivability Class

Tuesday:
AM & PM—State Certified Firefighter Survivability Class

Wednesday:
AM—Extinguishers
PM—Fireground Evolutions, EMS Scenarios, Fitness & Conditioning

Thursday:
AM & PM—Building Construction, How a House Works

Friday:
AM—Weekly Individual Performance Testing (IPT)—SCBA, Pre-Connect Hose Line, Search Operations, Tools Aloft, Axe use.
PM—Recruit Counseling, Skills Practice, EMS Scenarios, Fitness & Conditioning.

Week 6:

Monday:
AM—Large Area Search
PM—Fireground Evolutions, Fitness & Conditioning

Tuesday:
AM & PM—Auto Extrication

Wednesday:
AM & PM—Ventilation Operations

Thursday:
AM & PM—Forcible Entry

Friday:
AM—Midterm Written Exam, Weekly Individual Performance Testing (IPT)—SCBA, Pre-Connect Hose Line, Search Operations, Roof Ladder Aloft, Axe use, Knots & Slings.
PM—Recruit Counseling, Skills Practice, EMS Scenarios, Fitness & Conditioning, Online ICS classes: IS-100 and IS-700.

Week 7:

Monday:
AM & PM—Hazardous Materials First Responder Operational

Tuesday:
AM & PM—Hazardous Materials First Responder Operational

Wednesday:
AM & PM—ICS Class, I-200 (Basic ICS)

Thursday:
AM—ICS Class, I-200 (Basic ICS)
PM—Fireground Evolutions, EMS Scenarios, Fitness & Conditioning.

Friday:
AM—Weekly Individual Performance Testing (IPT)—Forward Lay, Search Operations, Tools Aloft, Axe use, Knots & Slings.
PM—Recruit Counseling, Skills Practice, EMS Scenarios, Fitness & Conditioning.

Week 8:

Monday:
AM & PM—Salvage & Overhaul, Fitness & Conditioning

Tuesday:
AM & PM—Rapid Intervention Crew Operations

Wednesday:
AM & PM—Master Streams, Aerial Operations, Fitness & Conditioning.

Thursday:
AM—Fire Investigation
PM—Fire Prevention

Friday:
AM—Weekly Individual Performance Testing (IPT)—SCBA, Pre-Connect Hose Line, Search Operations, Axe use, Knots & Slings.
PM—Recruit Counseling, Skills Practice, EMS Scenarios, Fitness & Conditioning.

Week 9:

Monday:
AM & PM—Wildland Firefighting (S-190 State Certified Class)

Tuesday:
AM & PM—Wildland Firefighting (S-130 State Certified Class)

Wednesday:
AM & PM—Wildland Firefighting (S-130 State Certified Class)

Thursday:
AM & PM—Wildland Firefighting (S-130 State Certified Class)

Friday:
AM & PM—Wildland Firefighting (S-130 State Certified Class)

Week 10:

Monday:
AM & PM—Live Fire Training, State Certified Fire Control 3B Class

Tuesday:
AM & PM—Live Fire Training, State Certified Fire Control 3B Class

Wednesday:
AM & PM—Live Fire Training, State Certified Fire Control 3B Class

Thursday:
AM—Scene Safety
PM—Utility Emergencies, Fitness & Conditioning

Friday:
AM—Weekly Individual Performance Testing (IPT)—SCBA, Pre-Connect Hose Line, Search Operations, Axe use, Knots & Slings.
PM—Recruit Counseling, Skills Practice, EMS Scenarios, Fitness & Conditioning.

Week 11:

Monday:
AM—County EMS Orientation
PM—Radio Communications, Fitness & Conditioning

Tuesday:
AM & PM—State Certified Confined Space Awareness

Wednesday:
AM—Public Education
PM—CPR Certification

Thursday:
AM & PM—CPR Instructor Training

Friday:
AM—Weekly Individual Performance Testing (IPT)—SCBA, Pre-Connect Hose Line, Roof Ladder Aloft, Search Operations, Axe use. PM—Recruit Counseling, Skills Practice, EMS Scenarios, Fitness & Conditioning.

Week 12:

Monday:
AM—Firehouse Software Training
PM—TeleStaff Training, Fitness & Conditioning

Tuesday:
AM—Final & Written Skills Review
PM—Skills Practice

Wednesday:
AM—Written Final Examination
PM—Fitness Final Testing

Thursday:
AM & PM—Individual Manipulative Skills Final Testing

Friday:

AM—Equipment Turn-In, Classroom & Drill Ground Clean-Up, Graduation Practice.

PM—Union Local BBQ, Graduation Ceremony

NOTE: The above subjects can change from department-to-department.

# # # #

**Remember—Don't Just Prepare For The
Test—Prepare For The Position!**

About the Author

Steve Prziborowski is a Deputy Chief with the Santa Clara County Fire Department (Los Gatos, CA), where he has served since 1995 in the following positions: Firefighter/Engineer-Paramedic, Fire Captain, Training Captain, Operations Captain, Battalion Chief, Battalion Chief/EMS Coordinator and now Deputy Chief overseeing Training, EMS, Emergency Preparedness, Community Education, the Volunteer Division and the Explorer Program. Steve has been in the fire service since 1992 when he began his career as an Associate Advisor with the Alameda Fire Department's Fire Explorer program, progressing to a position as a Student Firefighter with the Oakland Fire Department (a work experience program through Chabot College), and then as a paid-call Firefighter and paid-call Firefighter/Paramedic with the Elk Grove Fire Department prior to getting hired full-time with Santa Clara County Fire.

Steve has been an Adjunct Faculty member at Chabot College (Hayward, CA) since 1993. Steve spent seven years as the EMT Program Director and Primary Instructor, and almost five years as the Fire Technology Coordinator, and is currently the primary instructor for the Introduction to Fire Protection course. In addition to maintaining the Chabot College Fire Technology Program website—www.chabotfire. com, Steve also teaches oral interview preparation for the Firefighter 1 Academy.

Steve is recognized as a leading fire service instructor, was selected as the 2008 California Fire Service Instructor of the year and is a contributing editor to Firehouse.com. He is a Former President of the Northern California Training Officers Association, has completed the Executive Fire Officer Program at the National Fire Academy, and has received Chief Fire Officer Designation through the Commission on Professional Credentialing. He is a state-certified Chief Officer and Master Instructor, has earned a Master's degree in Emergency Services Administration, as well as a Bachelor's Degree in Criminal Justice and an Associate's Degree in Fire Technology.

Steve is currently a Program Planning Committee member for the International Association of Fire Chiefs Fire Rescue International Conference, as well as a member of a number of fire service organizations and associations. Steve has instructed, mentored and coached thousands of fire service personnel around the Country (current and future) of all ranks from Volunteer/Reserve Firefighter up to Fire Chief. He is a regular speaker and presenter at fire service events and conferences around the Country such as Firehouse Events, FDIC and the Fresno Symposium, and has authored numerous articles in all of the leading fire service publications such as Fire Engineering, Firehouse, Fire Rescue Magazine and Fire Chief, just to name a few.

To inquire about seminar or conference
presentations, please visit my websites at

www.chabotfire.com

and

www.code3firetraining.com

Lightning Source UK Ltd.
Milton Keynes UK
UKOW02f1157050816

280044UK00001B/244/P

9 781304 408808